I HEAR THE SOUND OF ABUNDANCE

A PROPHETIC DECREE
ON
THE PROPHETS REWARD
BY
DR. CHRISTIAN HARFOUCHE

DR. CHRISTIAN HARFOUCHE

I HEAR THE SOUND OF ABUNDANCE

FOREWORD BY
DR. JOHN AVANZINI

GLOBAL REVIVAL DISTRIBUTION
PENSACOLA, FLORIDA

Unless otherwise indicated, all scriptural references are from the *King James Version*, Cambridge, 1769.

For emphasis, the author has placed selected words from Bible quotations in italics and/or parenthesis.

I Hear the Sound of Abundance
ISBN 1-888966-71-8

Published by:
Global Revival Distribution
4317 N. Palafox St.
Pensacola, FL 32505
www.globalrevival.com

Cover & interior design and book production by:
M.E.D.I.A. Group
421 North Palafox Street, Pensacola, FL 32501
Cover illustration is protected by the 1976 United States Copyright Act.
Copyright © 2006 by M.E.D.I.A. Group, Inc

Copyright © 2006 Dr. Christian Harfouche. All rights reserved. Reproduction of text in whole or part without the express written consent by the author is not permitted and is unlawful according to the 1976 United States Copyright Act. Printed in the United States of America

And Elijah said unto Ahab, Get thee up, eat and drink; for there is a sound of abundance of rain.

1 Kings 18:41

DEDICATION

To the 7,000 Unsung Hero's who have not bowed the knee.

CONTENTS

FOREWORD — XI
by Dr. John Avanzini — xi

INTRODUCTION — XIII
Your Prophetic Invitation — xiii

CHAPTER 1 — 1
Principle 1: According to My Word, IT'S A DONE DEAL — 1
Blowing with the Wind of God — 3
Demonstrations and Manifestations — 6
All Things are Possible…to Those Who Believe — 9
Demonstrations of the Covenant — 11
Shepherds that Feed — 14
Anointed by Heaven to Change Earth — 15
The Corporate Call — 17
Feast, *not* Famine — 19
Signs, Wonders and Miracles — 22
Prophetic Fulfillment — 24
You will *not* Want — 28
The Place of Your Provision — 31
Go Show and Tell — 33

CHAPTER 2 — 35
Principle 2: Activation — 35
Activated for a Mission — 38
Draw from the Well — 40
God's Dream for Your Life — 44

CHAPTER 3 — 45
Principle 3: Specific Direction — 45
Specific Obedience — 49

CONTENTS

CHAPTER 4 — 51
Principle 4: Corporate Supply — 51
Fear Not, *Go* and *Do* — 54

CHAPTER 5 — 57
Principle 5: The All-Inclusive Anointing — 57
The Threshold of Breakthrough — 59
The Prophet's Reward — 63
Prophetic Declarations — 65
It is the Lord — 68
The Hundredfold Principle — 69
Ever-Increasing Abundance — 73
Unlimited Invitation — 76
Supernatural Results — 78
God's Best — 80
Testifying to Your Destiny — 82
YOU are the Testimony! — 85
Going to the Other Side — 88
Guarding Your Destiny — 91
It's BIGGER than You! — 94

CHAPTER 6 — 97
Principle 6: Confrontation and Demonstration — 97

CHAPTER 7 — 101
Principle 7: Divine Help — 101

CHAPTER 8 — 105
Principle 8: The Day of Showing — 105

CHAPTER 9 — 107
Principle 9: Revival Fire — 107
Revival and Restoration — 110

CONTENTS

Listen to the Sound	113
CHAPTER 10	**117**
Principle 10: *Run* Like Never Before!	117
Predestined Glory	120
The Sound that Moves You	122
Manifest Power	125
Work What You Hear	127
CHAPTER 11	**129**
I Hear the Sound of Abundance!	129
Together on the Frontline	135
Laugh in the Rain	138
PROPHETIC DECREE	**141**
Your Prophetic Word	141

FOREWORD
by Dr. John Avanzini

FRESH is a wonderful word because of the power that it brings to any word. For instance, there is *fresh* water, *fresh* air, or even a *fresh* revelation. FRESH REVELATION is especially powerful and true when it is used to describe the revelation that is found in Dr. Christian Harfouche's new book, *"I Hear the Sound of Abundance."*

For many years, the Body of Christ has been stirred by the possibilities that come to mind when we hear our Lord's promise in Matthew 10:41: *"He that receives a prophet in the name of a prophet shall receive a prophet's reward..."* However, specificity has been missing as to exactly *what* the *prophet's reward* really is. Well, wonder no more! There are *specific answers* for you in this powerful new book.

As always, we are taken by Dr. Harfouche to the most necessary ingredient of any encounter with God and the subsequent fulfillment of His promises. This key ingredient is the anointing. There must be an anointing present to activate the promises of God. That anointing always accompanies Dr. Harfouche, whether it is in his crusades, a church service, or even on a one-on-one encounter. The anointing is especially strong when you study the written revelations of this greatly anointed prophet and author.

Furthermore, an abundance of biblical proof always accompanies the words of revelation from Dr. Harfouche. This biblical proof powerfully authenticates that which he teaches. Also unique to the writings of Dr. Harfouche, is his divinely-directed ability to lead his reader into not only *knowing the truth*, but also, *possessing the promises* that God has extended.

GET READY for a most prosperous adventure! Not only will you receive a revelation of the prophet's reward, but you will also receive the reality of this reward manifested in *your* life.

Thank you Dr. Christian Harfouche for *another* great written explanation of the ABUNDANCE that God is ready to rain down on His children.

–Dr. John Avanzini, President
John Avanzini Ministries

INTRODUCTION
Your Prophetic Invitation

The life of Elijah offers a powerful glimpse of prophetic ministry in action. In fact, his life is a type and a shadow of what God has reserved for this end-time generation. It is a generation that is called to the frontlines of the greatest move of God the Earth has ever known

This corporate body of believers will experience the *all-inclusive* anointing of God's *unlimited* blessing. Like Elijah, they will hear the inaudible and step into a realm where the fire falls.

The people of God will testify to superabundance, never-failing performance and inexhaustible supply. Like a brilliant city, shining on a hill, Mount Zion, will represent *God's best*. Their testimony will be the envy of the world and *multitudes* will follow them into the Kingdom of Almighty God.

You are the generation that has been called by Heaven and this is the hour of your prophetic release! As you delve into the next ten principles of this prophetic *declaration*, God will open your ears to *hear* the prophetic *invitation*. Listen closely, the rain is just overhead and the skies are filling with the cloud of God's glory.

Dr. Christian Harfouche, President
Christian Harfouche Ministries Global Reach

1

PRINCIPLE 1
According to My Word, IT'S A DONE DEAL

> And Elijah the Tishbite who was of the inhabitants of Gilead, said unto Ahab, "As the Lord God of Israel liveth, before whom I stand, there shall not be dew nor rain these years, but according to my word."
>
> 1 Kings 17:1

Let's take a moment and picture Elijah. He was a hairy man who roamed the desert wearing his trademark leather girdle. When he was not walking, he was spending time with God, isolated in a cave. Always on the outskirts of society, he was impossible to track until he showed up with a Word from the Lord.

Elijah was born into a generation that was well established in its ways and nearly impossible to transform. This resistance to change was fostered by an unyielding governmental order and its tyrannical dignitaries. More specifically, the marriage between Ahab and Jezebel was the stronghold that bound the inhabitants of that land to its ungodly ways. Jezebel was the worshipper of Baal. She was an idolater and led a national campaign that promoted the worship of many gods. She came from what is now known as Southern Lebanon, or the Tyre and Sidon area. At that time, it was known as Northern Israel.

In the midst of this propaganda campaign, God raised up a prophet to say, *"As the Lord God of Israel liveth..."* Every other god was dead. Jezebel's other gods were not living. They were dumb idols, inanimate objects - void of life and powerless to perform.

During this time, Ahab erected a place of worship for Baal. The whole nation of Israel could worship whatever god they pleased. Idolatry was everywhere and the nation was rapidly being infiltrated by pagan influences. It is at precisely this point that Elijah, the leather-girdled, desert-roaming prophet appears. His message is cut and dry. It is direct and to the point.

Elijah said, *"As the Lord God of Israel liveth, before whom I stand, there shall not be dew nor rain these years, but according to my word"* (1 Kings 17:1b).

Blowing with the Wind of God

Notice Elijah said, *"according to my word."*

It's not a "might happen."
It's not a "could happen."
It was a **DONE DEAL**.

The outcome had already been established.

Elijah came prayed up. He didn't come with a "maybe" word. He came with a certain word. He came with an established word. He came with a direct Word from the Living God. It was already done.

Who do you think you are Elijah?
I am the messenger of the Living God.

What do you have?
I have a Word.

What good is that?
It is a DONE DEAL.
I have a NOW Word.
I have a POWER Word.
I have a MANIFESTATION Word.
I have a Word that is accompanied with miracles.
I have a Word that changes a nation.
I have a Word that changes the Earth.

Elijah said, *"...according to my word."* The word *"according"* in the Hebrew is *"peh."* It means, *"the mouth (as the means of blowing)."*

I Hear the Sound of Abundance

Ahab was ruling the land like he was in charge of the destiny of Israel. His actions and his methods resonated with *"This is how it is. I am King. My word is final."*

So, what message did Elijah bring to this idolatrous king and his queen?

Elijah said, *"Look, I serve the Living God and I stand before Him. There will not be dew or rain as by means of my blowing this Word."* In other words, *"For the next three and a half years, you will not see dew nor rain because **the Word I am speaking to you will keep on blowing. The only thing that will blow is what I have said.** This is the evidence that what I say stands. It is a done deal according to my word."*

The Word that stops the rain and the dew also brings the rain and the dew. It takes place through the means of *"blowing."*

All Scripture is God-breathed. It is alive and powerful because we serve a living and powerful God. We do not serve a dead God; therefore, we do not preach a dead sermon. We do not prophesy a dead Word. It is a living Word that is full of the life, breath and abundance of a Living God.

> THE ONLY WIND THAT YOU ARE GOING TO HEAR IS THE WIND OF THE REOCCURRING REMINDER OF GOD'S WORD. YOU ARE GOING TO BE VISITED TIME AND TIME AGAIN WITH ALL OF THE SUPERNATURAL HELP THAT YOU NEED, *ACCORDING TO MY WORD*.

"…According to my word"

Translation of *According* in Hebrew: *Peh*
Definition of *Peh*: The mouth (as the means of blowing).

The prophet Elijah proclaimed, *"There won't be dew or rain **according to what is blowing on you right now through my mouth.**"* When Elijah used *"according to my word,"* he was declaring the finality of it according to the inspiration of God. It was a God-breathed Word. It was a Word that settles the issue. It was a prophetic utterance and a divine decree. It was the final say.

When God speaks through His prophet and says, "...*according to my Word,*" you can be sure it's a done deal.

**This time in your life will be *according to my word.*
Heaven has given me the Word of the Lord for YOUR life.**

Demonstrations and Manifestations

> Elijah was a man subject to like passions as we are, and he prayed earnestly that it might not rain; and it rained not on the earth by the space of three years and six months. And he prayed again, and the heaven gave rain, and the earth brought forth her fruit.
>
> **James 5:17-18**

In the epistle referenced above, the writer speaks of a man that was caught up to Heaven. This was the same man that was lifted up in a whirlwind, called down fire from Heaven and performed great and mighty miracles. Elijah shook a whole nation and brought revival to a generation. So great was his reputation and influence that the nation of Israel almost idolized him. James writes, *"He was subject to like passions."* In other words, he was human and had the same encounters in life that everyday people face. This is not to say that Elijah was not a prophet or that he lacked power. James was simply underscoring the fact that Elijah was like you and me. What made him powerful was the fact that he prayed earnestly. The Bible says that Elijah prayed earnestly that it would not rain and it did not (James 5:17).

Jesus said, *"What things soever ye desire when ye pray, believe that ye receive them, and ye shall have them"* (Mark 11:24).

Elijah evidently believed that he received the answer to his prayer. He prayed that it would not rain and said, *"God, I know You heard me."* When Elijah went to go tell Ahab that it was not going to rain, it was already a done deal. It was already sealed. It was already settled. He was just informing the king of what had already taken place in the realm of the Spirit. *He was decreeing what had already come to pass.*

Demonstrations and Manifestations

> **What I am declaring to you today is not something that God is *going to do*. It is *already* a done deal. It has been unleashed. It has been released.**

"According to my word or by means of blowing."

Elijah prayed earnestly. He sought God during a season of death in his nation. It was a season of decline and stagnancy. Nothing was moving and the nation of Israel had settled into a pattern of despondency towards God. It looked like nothing could reach this lethargic people, but Elijah was well acquainted with a God of performance. He knew how to bring people to their knees. He knew how to prove that the God of Israel was not dead, but alive and powerful and working in their midst. Elijah had the ability to draw from God *demonstrations* and *manifestations*.

In the Greek language, the word **"demonstrations"** and the word **"manifestations"** are twins in the sense of meaning. Their definitions are very similar. They both can be defined in the following manner:

> To **show off**
> To **exhibit**
> To **demonstrate**
> To **accredit**
> To **approve**
> To **prove**
> To **set forth**
> To **show**

God is going to **ACCREDIT** what we preach
with validation of power.

God is going to **APPROVE** what we prophesy
with demonstration, manifestation, and performance.

<u>God will **PROVE** His Word.</u>

When Elijah delivered the prophetic Word, Ahab did not immediately believe it. This was of little consequence to the prophetic decree, for when Elijah said, *"according to my word"* and walked out, it was already a done deal. The miracle did not happen when he relayed the message to Ahab, it happened when he prayed earnestly.

It was a Word that was going to be demonstrated, proved, approved, accredited, and shown off as the prophetic Word for the hour. It was a Word that would be fulfilled in the ears of a people who had gone astray. Six million people in his nation were worshipping other gods, but Elijah knew where to go to stand before the Living God. He knew how to pray earnestly. He knew how to serve the God who would bring revival to the land and the rain of blessing to the nation.

> RIGHT NOW WE ARE IN THE MIDDLE OF THE GREATEST MANIFESTATION AND DEMONSTRATION OF THE BLESSING, DELIVERANCE, SALVATION, AND MIRACULOUS PERFORMANCE OF ALMIGHTY GOD.
>
> IT IS THE GREATEST HOUR.

Elijah stood praying and something *happened*.

All Things are Possible...to Those Who Believe

> And when he (Jesus) came to his disciples, he saw a great multitude about them, and the scribes questioning with them. And straightaway all the people when they beheld him were greatly amazed and running to him saluted him. And he asked the scribes, "What question ye them?" And one of the multitude answered and said, "Master, I have brought unto thee my son, which hath a dumb spirit; And wheresoever he taketh him, he teareth him; and he foameth, and gnasheth with his teeth, and pineth away; and I spake to thy disciples that they should cast him out; and they could not." He answered him, and saith, "O faithless generation, how long shall I be with you? How long shall I suffer you? Bring him unto Me." And they brought him unto Him; and when he saw Him, straightaway the spirit tare him; and he fell on the ground and wallowed foaming. And He asked his father, "How long is it ago since this came unto him?" And he said, "Of a child. And often times it hath cast him into the fire, and into the waters, to destroy him; but if thou can do any thing, have compassion on us, and help us."
>
> Mark 9:14-22

Most of the time, Jesus would not allow the demon spirits to manifest. Sometimes people think that without a manifestation, there is no deliverance, but this is not always true. In this situation, however, there is a very extreme manifestation. Since his childhood, this man has had a dumb spirit. The spirit *"teareth him...he foameth and gnasheth his teeth and pineth away."*

The God who continually supplied supernatural help through the ministry of Christ and who demonstrated His power through the early Church, has not vacated His position of performance. He has not turned humanity over to their own methods of self-help.

It is foolish to think that God does not supply supernatural help.
It is foolish to think that deliverance does not belong to us today.
It is foolish to think that the power of God is not available.
It is foolish to proclaim, *"The day of miracles is over."*

Foolish statements that deny the power of a Living God are evidence of ignorance, not qualification for ministry.

Jesus said unto him, "If thou canst believe, all things are possible to him that believeth."

Mark 9:23

ALL THINGS are possible *to them that believe.* The prerequisite for "all things" is to believe.

Demonstrations of the Covenant

What are YOU believing?

Is it the Word of God or is it *SOMETHING ELSE*?
Is Jesus the Miracle Worker for *TODAY*?
Is His blessing on you *RIGHT NOW*?
Does His Word equal a *DONE DEAL* in your life?

What do you LISTEN to?

These are important questions to ask yourself.
What you listen to will determine your results in life.

So then faith cometh by hearing and hearing by the Word of God.

Romans 10:16-18

CHOOSE TO LISTEN to nothing but the goodness of God.
CHOOSE TO LISTEN to nothing but the Word of God.
CHOOSE TO LISTEN to nothing but the right music.
CHOOSE TO LISTEN to nothing but the right thoughts.

CHOOSE **TO LISTEN**
to the inspired promise that is a done deal.

> IN THE MIND OF GOD, THIS TIME, THIS HOUR…IS *DONE*.
> IT IS A DONE DEAL.
>
> ACCORDING TO MY WORD = IT'S A **DONE DEAL**.

**Do not allow *anything* to blow in your life
except the breath of God.**

> **For I am not ashamed of the gospel of Christ; for it is the power of God unto salvation to every one that believeth...**
>
> **Romans 1:16a**

Everyone is included on the blessing. All you have to do is believe. However, this does not mean that you can have what you want by believing for *whatever*. People come to church and stand in the prayer line with an attitude of, "*God, all I want is what you have for me.*" This might sound humble, but God wants you to be specific. Find out what He has promised and believe for it specifically. This is pleasing to God.

To the father of the child, Jesus said, "*If thou canst believe, all things are possible to him that believeth*" (Mark 9:23b).

"*All things are possible*" does not mean that you can have a new wife, a new son, or trade in a family member for a better model! Jesus was saying that we can be *specific* because we will *specifically* get what we are believing God for.

This principle will put the dynamite of Almighty God in your life. It will put the nitroglycerin of the Holy Ghost in your mouth. When you launch out in your words, they will explode with demonstrations of the covenant. People will see the child of God walking with the authoritative anointing that Jesus has delegated.

> It is happening right now.
> It is already a done deal.
> There are no options.
> We are taking no prisoners.
> We do not make prisoners.
> We are setting the captive free.
> We are letting God's people go.
> We are raising up an army.
> We are raising up a family.

We are building the House of the Almighty God.

ACCORDING TO MY WORD.

Shepherds that Feed

The father of the child was believing specifically. He believed that Jesus was going to have compassion on his child but he wanted Jesus to help his unbelief.

How does God help our unbelief?

He gives us shepherds that feed us and we shall fear no more.

And I will set up shepherds over them which shall feed them; and they shall fear no more, nor be dismayed, neither shall they be lacking, saith the Lord.

Jeremiah 23:4

God sends a mouth to blow into your life a Word that will continue to work day and night. This Word will work the invisible into manifestation and materialization. It will work to perform in your life. It will overcome and overwhelm you because *you only know what you know*. The revelation you have is smaller than the revelation He has. **What is coming to you is EXCEEDINGLY ABUNDANTLY above all that you could ever ask or think.**

Now unto Him that is able to do EXCEEDINGLY ABUNDANTLY above all that we ask or think, according to the power that worketh in us.

Ephesians 3:30

Anointed by Heaven to Change Earth

> When Jesus saw that the people came running together, he rebuked the foul spirit, saying unto him, "Thou dumb and deaf spirit, I charge thee, come out of him, and enter no more into him." And the spirit cried, and rent him sore, and came out of him, and he was as one dead; insomuch that many said, "He is dead." But Jesus took him by the hand, and lifted him up; and he arose. And when he was come into the house, his disciples asked him privately, "Why could not we cast him out?" And He said unto them, "This kind can come forth by nothing, but by prayer and fasting."
>
> **Mark 9:25-29**

Jesus rebuked the foul spirit with a Word. The disciples were already well practiced in casting out devils, but they could not cast this one out. This spirit trespassed the boy's body. What was intended by God to be the temple of the Holy Ghost, was invaded by devils. There was seemingly no one who had the ability to help this young man. All human remedies were powerless to perform.

Thank God that Jesus gave us the ability to eject devils!

Heaven has given you
the free **GIFT**
the free **ABILITY**
the free **ANOINTING** and
the free **AUTHORITY**
to do something about the unclean!

You are a **LIBERATOR!**
You are a **DELIVERER!**

You are anointed by Heaven to change Earth!

People thought the boy died, but he was actually under the power of God. I have had people in my meetings that were so gone in God that they had to be carried home. How is it that some people still ask, "Where is *that* in the Bible?"

The demonic nonsense stopped when the enemy left. He lay motionless and many people feared that he was dead.

The One with the Word said to the Bondage and the Binder, "*Leave him. Come out of him and do not enter him anymore.*" The Word drove out the unclean spirit and brought immediate deliverance. When the man was freed and powerless, Jesus lifted him up and imparted strength into him.

Do you want the key that will make every word in your life explosive?

According to my word = It is a done deal.

Did you see Jesus fast or pray during any part of this story?

No, you did not. This means that what Jesus DID, made it a DONE DEAL. Jesus had already prayed. He had already fasted. When He came face to face with the impossible, it had already been dealt with. It was a done deal. This is why *according to my word* equals *it is a done deal*.

> IN YOUR LIFE, *IT* IS A DONE DEAL.
> THERE IS FAITH COMING INTO YOUR LIFE AT THIS VERY MOMENT.
> THIS FAITH WILL MOVE YOUR MOUNTAINS
> AND RAISE UP YOUR VALLEYS.
> IT IS A LIFE-CHANGING ANOINTING.
> IT IS A YOKE-BREAKING ANOINTING.

The power of Almighty God is upon you NOW and you will never be the same.

The Corporate Call

God's Word is clear about you.

You are a *chosen generation.*
You are a *royal priesthood.*
You are a *holy nation.*
You are a *peculiar people.*

Before I formed you in the belly, I knew you…..and before you came out of the womb, I ordained you...

Jeremiah 1:5a

You did not just show up on planet Earth. God has already predestined you. He has foreknown you.

You are part of a **CHOSEN GENERATION**
that Heaven has planned,
that Hell cannot defeat,
that Earth cannot stop,
that the planet cannot change,
and that circumstance cannot defy.

> GOD GOT A HOLD OF YOU AND GOD WILL CONTINUE
> TO INFLUENCE, INJECT, AND IMPLEMENT
> HIS POWER IN YOUR LIFE.
> TODAY, YOU ARE GOING FROM ONE LEVEL TO ANOTHER.

Elijah was a shadow and a type of days planned for a corporate people. He was the forerunner to a generation that will blaze the Earth with a Heaven-sent Word. This generation will walk in the boldness of agreement. They will carry an internal mandate and a corporate unction that will direct their hearts into prophetic destiny. They will rise up with one voice and broadcast a Word to a world that is filled with darkness and confusion. That Word will pierce the darkness and will herald the dawning of a new day.

This generation will rise up with a good word, a victorious word, *a God Word*. They will begin with *revival* and continue into *restoration*.

> They will:
> *embarrass* the adversary,
> *frustrate* the enemy,
> *drive back* the opposition,
> *move* the mountains,
> *do* the impossible,
> *see* the invisible and
> *hear* the inaudible.

This is a generation with a purpose.

It is a people that will say, *"I know that God has more for me than what religion has taught."* It is a generation that will say, *"My God is not a past tense God or a future tense God. My God is a NOW God."*

Feast, *not* Famine

Elijah entered the world scene when nothing seemed to be happening. Idolatry and personal opinion were rampant. There was discord and disharmony within the nation. Everyone had their own opinion. Everyone saw it his or her own way. The lines between right and wrong had become blurred. What was once black and white, had now become a murky gray. What was objective in nature, had become subjective in the sight of all.

In the midst of this, God sent *an anointing* and *an anointed vessel* to bring His blessing to His people.

> AS YOU CONTINUE TO STUDY THE PROPHETIC DECLARATION WITHIN THESE PAGES, YOU WILL BEGIN TO SEE WHAT GOD HAS FOR THIS END-TIME GENERATION.

Jesus said, *"It is finished. It is paid in full!"*

The deal is done.
The devil is dusted.
Hell is defeated.
Man is redeemed.
The blessings are procured.
Salvation is available.
Healing belongs to you.
Prosperity is the order of the day.

I will build My Church and the gates of hell shall not prevail against it.

Matthew 16:18b

It is *finished*.
It is a *done deal*.

God anointed Elijah to come and to literally bring a famine just to get man's attention.

There was a day when you were no longer satisfied with the status quo. What had filled you, suddenly lacked substance. What you were accustomed to, no longer fed you. It did not satisfy. It did not fulfill. It felt like famine.

Today, God does not have a famine in store for you.
He has a feast in store for you!

He has the **victory** beyond the battle.
He has a **feast** beyond the famine.
He has **abundance** beyond the hunger.
He has **strength** beyond the weakness.
He has **vindication, promotion** and **blessing...**
for your life and home.

There is not one person who is reading this that is a bad person. In fact, from the perspective of Heaven, there are only two types of people in the Earth. There are those that God has already got a hold of and then there are those that God wants to get a hold of.

It doesn't matter *where* you are right now.
It doesn't matter *what* you did yesterday.

When God gets a hold of you, He will change your life forever. He will not stop with the famine. He will send the rain. He will send the food. He will release His abundance into your life.

He is sending *revival*, but He will not stop with revival. He is sending *restoration*.

He is going to bless your home. He is going to bless your life. He is going to anoint you. He is going to equip you. He is going to empower you. He is going to inject you. He is going to send you. He is going to use you.

There is not one bad person.
There is not a person that can't measure up
to the expectation of God.

Elijah was a man subject to like passions, *yet* he prayed earnestly.

Study this key: Elijah took time aside. He went away by himself. He left the standard and the status quo. He moved away from the multitudes and spent time with God. This is not a call to become a hermit and to dwell in the desert. This is a *prophetic call* to a *chosen generation* to set aside time for prayer, worship, gathering and connection in God. As you do this, you will hear from Heaven. The sound that you will hear will move you and change you. The force of it will echo throughout the very fiber of your being. It will bring you into synch with God's declaration over your life.

Signs, Wonders and Miracles

Elijah walked into Ahab's court and pronounced what had already been done. The river was still flowing, crops were still thriving and the ground may still have been moist from a previous rain. Yet, Elijah stood before Ahab with a prophetic decree. The prophet knew what had already been accomplished. **It was a done deal in prayer.**

Elijah said, *"Shut Heaven. Bring a demonstration and a manifestation."*

Demonstration.
It is to *show off*.

Manifestation.
It is to *exhibit*.

God will exhibit in your life. The natural people of the Earth demand natural evidence. *"I will believe it when I see it"* is the reoccurring sentiment of the natural realm.

No problem with that! We do not serve an absent landlord!

HE IS HERE!

He is *here* to bless.
He is *here* to heal.
He is *here* to raise up.

We serve the God of the now.
We serve the God of the hour.
We serve the good God.
We serve the only true and wise God.

There is no problem with exhibition. God will exhibit. He will demonstrate. He will accredit His Word. He will approve His Word *and* His messengers.

Jesus of Nazareth, a man approved of God among you by miracles and wonders and signs which God did by Him in the midst of you all.

Acts 2:22

God is going to SHOW OFF in your life.
God is going to DEMONSTRATE in your life.
God is going to ACCREDIT Himself in your life.
God is going to VALIDATE His presence.

You will walk in the Word. You will take what God said, hold onto His Word, and He will accredit your life with evidence. People will see evidence in your life. They will see accreditation.

This is God's love for humanity.

You will be approved of God. God's Word will be proven in your life with an immediate performance.

Demonstration.
Manifestation.

There will be a setting forth. You will be set apart. You will be seen as someone who has supernatural help. It will not just be a leather-bound book or some notes. They will witness and recognize something in your life that supersedes natural ability.

God is going to set you apart.

Prophetic Fulfillment

Ahab, oblivious to his own delusions, looked around his ivory palace and admired its stately beauty. His treasuries were full and everything seemed great. Of course, the nation was in bondage and the people were lost in idolatry. These trivialities, however, were inconsequential to the king and his queen. Life was royal, with the exception of the leather-girdled prophet that had shown up in his court.

Elijah, on the other hand, looked around and saw Ahab humbled, Jezebel judged and the nation revived. When Elijah came and delivered the Word of the Lord, it was already a done deal. It didn't matter what the circumstance looked like! It didn't matter what the palace looked like. He had heard from Heaven.

Elijah informed Ahab, *"... according to my word."*

The prophet proclaimed the Word of the Lord.

It was a DONE DEAL.

Perhaps Ahab said to himself, *"Well, we will see."*

One week may have passed. No sign of dew. No sign of rain. The king wasn't too concerned though. *"It's just coincidence,"* he thought. Besides, he had enough water. He had enough wine. He had enough food to hold a palace feast. There was no hint of famine. The pangs of it could not be felt, yet it was already a *done deal*.

The famine starts when there is no rain and the fruit of the Earth fails to produce. Only when there is no water for the sheep and no feed for the cattle, does reality set in. It's famine time. The ground has become cracked and parched. There is no fruit, no bread, no wheat, and no barley. All of a sudden, the things that men boast in become the very evidence of their shame.

Lack is not evidence of a move of God. Lack is just simply moving *towards* a move of God. This is very important to understand.

The people of the Earth today have been taught by experience and conditioned by nature to accept the conditions of the economy, the present world order, their situation in life, where they live, how they live and what they will do to "make do." We have been taught to accept the hardness of an unyielding, natural world. Famine, however, *does not* apply to the child of God. It *does not* apply to you.

Elijah prayed strongly because he *believed* that he was called. He believed that he was serving a reliable God. He was convinced that God would take care of him. If he prophesied a famine and was not worried about it, then he must have had a good reason! He must have been confident in his God!

Do not read about perilous times and become afraid!
Do not read about the anti-Christ and get nervous!
Do not read the report and get paranoid!

Why the peace? Why the confidence? Why the security?

Rest in the understanding that God has His plan for your life. The circumstances of the world *do not apply to you.* Famine is *not* your testimony. Your testimony is, *"Oh yes, my God did exceedingly abundantly above all that I could ever ask or think."* ABUNDANCE is your testimony!

After Elijah delivered the Word, he walked out into a realm where his word was a done deal. It was a God-breathed Word. It was a prophetic Word. For the next three and a half years, he said, *"Nothing will come from Heaven. You will only have the echo and the breath of my word ringing in your ears until you are ready to accept a revival from God."*

Elijah walked out into that realm and God said, *"Go to the brook because I have commanded the ravens to feed you there."* The name *"Elijah"* is translated, *"My God is Jehovah."*

So he went and did according to the word of the Lord: for he went and dwelt by the brook...and the ravens brought him bread and flesh in the morning and bread and flesh in the evening; and he drank of the brook.

1 Kings 17:5a, 6

Is your God, Jehovah?
Is your Savior, Jesus?

If He is, then He has commanded things to feed you. He has commanded you to be fed. He has commanded you to have a brook. He has commanded blessing in the middle of famine, supply in the middle of drought, abundance in the middle of lack, and provision in the middle of need.

He directed Elijah where to go.

There is no reason to fear because you serve a reliable God. You serve a faithful God. You serve a God of superabundant supply.

Remember, when you *rely*, He is *able*.

God did not tell Elijah to go to the brook *before* he delivered the word. He had to step out into the God-realm, the faith-realm. Here is a man that has been sent to declare famine to a nation, yet he does not worry about himself! He knows the God he is serving.

We know what kind of a God we are serving. He is not going to leave you out. He is not going to leave you without. He is not going to leave you where you are today.

He has a place of appointment, revival, and restoration for your life. He has direction for you, even in the midst of the most insurmountable circumstance. He has made a way for you. He has made provision for those whose God is Jehovah.

How are you going to be fed Elijah? You have your own brook and you have ravens that bring you both bread and meat in the morning and in the evening.

Elijah experienced **ABUNDANCE** during the famine.

If birds can fly in food in the Old Covenant, then planes can fly in the food in the New Covenant. Trucks can drive in the food!

> You are not going to *just* have your **NEED** met.
> You are going to have your **WANT** met!

You shall not WANT *for anything*!

There's always SUPERABUNDANCE for God's people!

You will *not* Want

Do what God tells you to do. If God says, *"Climb out on a limb,"* do it. Follow His voice. If God sends you to raise up people to step out into the faith-realm, then tell them what God has told you. If God tells you to equip the people that will be on the front lines of His blessing, then do it. If He sends you to them, go to them. Go to them like we are going to you.

We are preparing you for what God has for you. This is the hour for the great and glorious end-time family of believers. This is not a fantasy, but this is something that is biblical. We have already prayed through. We have already heard from Heaven. It is a done deal.

Whether we have met you or not, we continually pray for every partner, member, friend, and associate around the world. If you are connected to the Lord and Savior or if you want to be, then this is your time to step into prophetic fulfillment. You will not only have your *needs* met, but you will have your *wants* met. You will have the superabundance of God.

You will not *want* for anything.

Your ministry, your call, your life, your family, your business will not "want" to expand and not have the resources. You will not "want" to do better, but not have the ability. You will not "want" to have a greater anointing to serve God, but not have the capacity.

You will have what you want. God will supply for every good work in your life. You will walk in the realm of "exceedingly abundantly above all." *You will testify to abundance!*

And the word of the Lord came unto him saying, "Get

thee hence, and turn thee eastward, and hide thyself by the brook Cherith, that is before Jordan. And it shall be, that thou shalt drink of the brook; and I have commanded the ravens to feed thee there." So he went and did according unto the Word of the Lord; for he went and dwelt by the brook Cherith that is before Jordan. And the ravens brought him bread and flesh in the morning, and bread and flesh in the evening; and he drank of the brook. And it came to pass after a while, that the brook dried up, because there had been no rain in the land.

1 Kings 17:2-7

People have a hard time believing this because it is not sensible, but somebody has to be bold enough to believe the Word of God! Intelligent people will read about ravens flying in food and not believe it. The religious crowd has been attending church for years, but has never seen a miracle. They have never seen the tangible expression of God. They are not acquainted with the God of power, but have been programmed not to think, not to expect and not to believe. Their convictions are buried in their traditions.

What would make someone believe that birds fed a man?

They have to be convinced. The *"I will believe it when I see it crowd"* needs natural evidence.

Our confession is not, "Our God *was* Jehovah."
No, our God *is* Jehovah!

He is the same yesterday, today and forever.

Hebrew 13:8

We believe it because it still happens.
God still makes a way where there is no way.

He still saved your life when there was no hope. He still delivered you out of the hand of the adversary. He still preserved you when people thought you would not make it. He brought you farther than you expected, *but He has only just begun.*

**He is about to do MORE in your life
than you have ever anticipated or expected.**

God is accrediting His Word with signs following.

**We serve
THE GOD OF THE HAPPENINGS.**

The Place of Your Provision

Elijah did not run and hide because ravens were flying his way! He did what God said and lived by the brook. The whole nation was in famine. Everybody was in famine, but Elijah was living by the brook. He did not have to search for food. He was living in divine supply. The provision had to go to where he was. The abundance had to follow him.

WHEREVER YOU ARE,
is where the **blessing** is coming.

WHEREVER GOD HAS DIRECTED YOU,
is where the **provision** is being sent.

WHEREVER GOD HAS PLACED YOU,
is where you are going to be **visited**, **blessed**, and **touched**.

WHEREVER HE HAS SENT YOU,
is where the **abundance** is.

Elijah lived by the brook. The nation was in famine. Millions of people were having famine for dinner, but Elijah was having something different. He was living under a different economy. *Why?* His God *is* Jehovah.

Your *economy is different* than the Earth's economy.
Your *conditions are different* than the Earth's conditions.
Your *dwelling place is different* than those of the world.

And the word of the Lord came unto him saying, "Arise, get thee to Zarephath, which belongeth to Zidon, and dwell there: behold I have commanded a widow woman there to sustain thee." So he arose and went to Zarephath. And when he came to the gate of the city, behold, the

widow woman was there gathering of sticks; and he called to her, and said, "Fetch me, I pray thee, a little water in a vessel that I may drink."

1 Kings 17:8

The Word of the Lord came to Elijah. *"There will not be dew or rain, according to my word."*

Every time the Word came to Elijah, it came to tell him what God had already done. It was a done deal. God said, *"I have already commanded the ravens, now go let them minister to you. I have already appointed a place by the brook. Go there now. When you arrive at the next point, I will have already made preparation for you by commanding the widow woman to sustain you."*

When the Word of the Lord comes to you, He does not come to tell you what He is going to do, He comes to tell you what He has ALREADY PREPARED.

The table is already spread. We are just hearing about it.
The feast is already on. We are just reading about it.
The victory is already won. We are just partaking of it.

<u>IT IS A DONE DEAL</u>.

He **already** took care of what has threatened you.
He **already** took care of the lies that were said about you.
He **already** took care of what opposed you, resisted you and tried to defeat you.

Your victory is imminent. Your provision is secured.

His Word to you is, *"IT IS A DONE DEAL."*

Go Show and Tell

Jesus came into the earth realm to bless all.

How God anointed Jesus of Nazareth with the Holy Ghost and with power who went about doing good, and healing all that were oppressed of the devil, for God was with Him.

Acts 10:38

It was God's will to heal everyone. Jesus came with an anointing to heal all. The Bible says that the eyes of the Lord (the Spirit of the Lord) run to and fro throughout the whole Earth. He is perusing the planet; looking for a man or a woman whose heart is perfect (mature) and on whose behalf He can show Himself mighty (Zechariah 4:10).

Today, God is literally looking. He is looking for those who will allow Him to demonstrate in their lives. He wants to show Himself mighty on *your* behalf.

Till we all come in the unity of the faith, and the knowledge of the Son of God, unto a perfect man.

Ephesians 4:13

God has been looking for the corporate people that will accept this word of blessing. He has been looking for the generation that will rise up and receive His promises. His eyes have been searching for those who will allow Him to show Himself mighty and to perform on their behalf.

You better get ready.
It is not *going* to happen...

IT IS A DONE DEAL.

What can God do for a perfect man?
He can show Himself **MIGHTY** on their behalf.

God is going to show off your life.

God was looking for many widows to bless. He would have liked to show Himself mighty in many lives. Only one widow, however, was qualified for this kind of visitation. Only one widow was qualified for **supernatural abundance**. *Only one widow received the prophetic Word as a **done deal**.* Recognizing the Word of the Lord, she joined herself to the Word by coming into agreement with the Word.

> IF YOU ARE JOINED TO THIS WORD, YOU AND YOUR HOUSEHOLD WILL STEP INTO AND ENJOY BLESSING AND ABUNDANCE BECAUSE OF THE COVENANT THAT GOD HAS WITH YOU.

Elijah was a prophet, appointed by God. He was sent to bless the widow woman and to speak into her life. This is how God sent him: *"I have commanded HER to sustain YOU."*

When the anointed, the anointing,
the Word of God comes to your area,
and God gives you the privilege to sustain it,
IT IS FOR THE PURPOSE OF SUSTAINING <u>YOU</u>!

God told the prophet, *"I have commanded the woman to sustain you there."* You know the end of the story. Elijah ended up giving her a word that took her limited resources and made them permanent provision until the time of visitation.

The economy that belonged to one man,
spread to another life because God sent Him.

This means that God does not just bless the man that He calls, God also blesses the man that He sends.

2

PRINCIPLE 2
Activation

Elijah found the widow woman that God had sent him to. She was gathering sticks, preparing to cook her very last meal. It was famine and she was getting ready to die.

Elijah *saw her* and *knew her* by the Holy Ghost.

And the word of the Lord came unto him saying, "Arise, get thee to Zarephath, which belongeth to Zidon, and dwell there: behold I have commanded a widow woman there to sustain thee." So he arose and went to Zarephath. And when he came to the gate of the city, behold, the widow woman was there gathering of sticks; and he called to her, and said, "Fetch me, I pray thee, a little water in a vessel that I may drink." And as she was going to fetch it, he called to her, and said, "Bring me, I pray thee, a morsel of bread in thine hand."

1 Kings 17:8-11

The first words out of his mouth can be summed up in the second principle: ACTIVATION.

Activation. God will activate you. He will give you an impartation for ACTIVITY that will bring PRODUCTIVITY into your life.

Elijah did not walk up to the woman and say, *"Hi. My name is Elijah and my God is Jehovah, IF you bring me some water."*

Elijah spoke a word. He did not attempt an introduction or

even a brief list of his qualifications. It was of little consequence.

When you know the anointing, you do not need a handshake first. You do not need the formalities of an introduction. You do not need a letter of recommendation.

When you know the anointing,
you do not close the book.

When you know the anointing,
you do not flip the channel.

When you know the anointing,
you do not walk out of the meeting.

When you know the anointing,
you do not doubt the promise.

When you know the anointing, you get ACTIVATED.
When you get activated, you are ready for the ACTIVITY that will bring the PRODUCTIVITY into your life.

The Word comes carrying the *breath* of God. It is a Word of command. It is a Word of activation.

No explanations.
No introductions.

The widow woman didn't ask, *"Who are you? Where did you come from?"*

The wisdom of God knew. *"There is a widow woman that has been praying to Me and I told her, 'There is a visitation coming.' She does not know exactly how it is coming to her, but when it comes, the confirmation of it will jump up in her spirit. This will be more than enough to let her know that her day of revival and restoration has come."*

The witness will be more than enough.

The very words on this page bear witness within your spirit. You are not ignorant of the affirmation and confirmation of this prophetic decree.

You are living in the day when
Heaven will vindicate.
Heaven will bless.
Heaven will restore.

Heaven will fill every area of your life with God's best.

YOU ARE BEING ACTIVATED.

You are in the middle of a move of God.

Activated for a Mission

As she was going to fetch the water, he asked her for bread. She immediately went to do what he said. *Why? The prophet had activated her.*

> YOU HAVE BEEN ACTIVATED.
> YOU ARE ON YOUR WAY TO PRODUCTIVITY.
> YOU ARE ON YOUR WAY TO INCREASE.
> YOU ARE ON YOUR WAY TO RESTORATION.
> YOU ARE IN THE *MIDDLE* OF YOUR VISITATION.

In the original language, the word *"fetch"* means, *"bring me."* It is the word *"lakash"* in the Hebrew. It means, *"to take in the widest variety of applications."*

In other words, Elijah told her, *"Go and bring some water, buy some water, carry away some water, draw some water, get some water, receive some water, seize some water, send for some water, take away some water, or win some water. Put it in a vessel and bring it to me."*

Elijah saw the widow woman for the first time at the city gate. God immediately spoke to him and said, *"That is the woman that I have commanded to sustain you."*

Opening his mouth, Elijah turned to the woman and said, *"Go and do whatever it takes to get some water. Bring it to me so that I may drink."* The woman turned around to do as he said.

Activation is not when they put something on you. Activation is not when somebody hypnotizes you or influences you.

Activation is God turning on what was dormant.
YOU HAVE BEEN ACTIVATED.

Activated for a Mission

The capacity for God results has been dormant in your life.

Why?

You have needed this Word of **revelation**. You have needed that which has now been **sent** to inform you of what is *already* a **done deal**.

The thing that was designed by God to work in your life, has now been **activated and released into productivity.**

This activation does not come from the *outside*. It comes from *within*. This is how you know, that you know, that you know, THAT YOU KNOW.

"Do whatever you have to do to bring me water in a vessel to drink."

What did the widow woman do? She brought the water!

She was activated for a mission.

> YOU ARE ON A MISSION TO FULFILL SOMETHING GOD HAS FOR YOU.
> IT IS A TIME OF FOCUS. IT IS A TIME OF APPOINTMENT.
> IT IS A TIME OF REVIVAL AND A TIME OF RESTORATION.

Your activation for this mission is the most specific and relevant activity in your life.

Draw from the Well

> Then cometh he to a city of Samaria, which is called Sychar, near to the parcel of ground, that Jacob gave to his son Joseph. Now Jacob's well was there, Jesus therefore, being wearied with his journey, sat thus on the well, and it was about the sixth hour. There cometh a woman of Samaria to draw water; Jesus saith to her, "Give me to drink." Then saith the woman of Samaria unto Him, "How is it that thou, being a Jew, asketh drink of me, which am a woman of Samaria? For the Jews have no dealings with the Samaritans." Jesus answered and said unto her, "If you knew the gift of God, and who it is that saith to thee, 'Give me to drink,' thou wouldest have asked of him, and he would have given thee living water."
>
> John 4:5-10

Jesus did not introduce Himself. He did not say who He was. He did not tell her where He came from. He did not even mention what might happen if she obeyed, but God had an appointment with this woman.

The Jew that should not speak to a Samaritan spoke a command that brought her into blessing. She had an appointment. She was at the right place, at the right time.

Jesus said to the woman, *"I am just activating you. What you are going to do is NATURAL, but what I have to give is SUPERNATURAL. I cannot bring you My supernatural unless I bring to you a revelation of Who you are dealing with. If you knew Who was talking to you, and the gift of God that is before you, you would have asked of Him, and He would have given you living water."*

Taken aback by the words of this man, the woman pointed out the obvious. *"Sir, the well is deep and you have nothing to draw this 'living water' up with."* After all, she thought, *"I have my vessel. I have my own means of drawing water up out of the well, yet He passes through my town and offers me this 'living water'?"*

Still holding her water pot, the woman said to Jesus, *"How are you going to give me 'living water'? It seems to me that I have the vessel. I have the well. I have the ability to draw water and You do not. How are You going to give me this water? Are You greater than our father Jacob, which gave us this well? This well has been in this parcel of land for hundreds and hundreds of years. We have been supplied for and we are accustomed to coming here. I have what is necessary to draw water, so how is it that You are promising a greater blessing? Are You greater than Jacob who gave us this well?"*

> **Jesus said unto her, "Whosoever drinketh of this water shall thirst again; But whosoever drinketh of the water that I shall give him shall never thirst. But the water that I shall give him shall be in him a well of water springing up into everlasting life." The woman saith unto Him, "Sir, give me this water, that I thirst not, neither come hither to draw." Jesus saith unto her, "Go call thy husband, and come hither." The woman answered and said, "I have no husband." Jesus said unto her, "Thou hast well said, I have no husband. For thou hast had five husbands; and he whom thou now hast is not thy husband; in that saidst thou truly." The woman saith unto Him, "Sir, I perceive thou art a prophet. Our fathers worshipped in this mountain; and ye say, that in Jerusalem is the place where men ought to worship."**
>
> **John 4:13-20**

Jesus said, *"You are impressed with the least. You are impressed with what wears out. You are impressed with what never fully satisfies. You are impressed with the lesser blessing. Your eyes are on the easy stuff. You think the easy stuff is greater than the God stuff. You do not know that if you drink this water, you are going to be thirsty again. But whosoever that drinks the water that I shall give him shall never thirst. The water I shall give him shall be in him a well, springing up into everlasting life! What you give to Me is something that is exhaustible. What I give to you is something that is abundant and always satisfies. When you drink of the well of salvation, it will keep on springing up unto everlasting life. You will never have to have a sad day when you remember that you have been redeemed. The joy of the Lord is your strength."*

He has the greater blessing for *your* life.

The first words that Jesus spoke to the Samaritan were, *"Give me to drink."* This was not an accident. The Word of God Himself was also well versed in the reading of the Scriptures. Jesus always told people, *"Did you not read the Bible? Didn't you read the Word? Didn't you read 'where it says'?"*

Jesus knew how He, *as the Word of God*, supplied for the Old Testament widow woman. He also knew how He, *as a man anointed by the Holy Ghost*, would supply for the woman at the well. **Jesus activated each of them for a mission.**

After a few words were exchanged, this woman came to the conclusion that Jesus knew an awful lot about the intimate details of her life. She said to Him, *"I perceive Thou art a prophet."*

Jesus saith unto her, "Woman, believe Me, the hour cometh, when ye shall neither in this mountain, nor yet at Jerusalem, worship the Father. Ye worship ye know not what; we know what we worship; for salvation is of the Jews. But the hour cometh, and now is, when the true worshippers shall worship the Father in spirit and in truth; for the Father seeketh such to worship him. God is a Spirit, and they that worship him must worship in spirit and in truth." The woman saith unto Him, "I know that Messiah cometh, which is called Christ; when He is come, He will tell us all things." Jesus saith

unto her, "I that speak unto thee am He." And upon this came his disciples, and marvelled that He talked with the woman, yet no man said, "What seekest thou?" or "Why talkest thou with her?" The woman then left her water pot, and went her way into the city, and saith to the men, "Come, see a man, which told me all things that ever I did, is not this the Christ?" Then they went out of the city, and came unto him.

John 4:21-29

The woman left her water pot. She did not draw water out for Jesus. She said, *"Go ahead. I do not know how much you want to drink. Keep the water pot. Drink all day. Drink all night because I just found something that is greater than this well and my water pot."*

"I have been activated for a mission. I have found the One," heralded the woman.

The woman left the water pot because she was activated for a mission. She found the One that is the problem-solver. She went and told everybody that she had found Somebody. She left her water pot. *"You can drink the whole well for all I care! I am going to go and tell everybody in Samaria that I have found a Man. Come see a Man that told me everything."* She was activated.

> YOU ARE BEING ACTIVATED FOR A MISSION,
> FOR A SUPERNATURAL MINISTRY,
> FOR THIS TIME OF PROPHETIC DESTINY.

God's Dream for Your Life

In this hour, you are living in the middle of the fulfillment of God's dream for your life. You are standing in the prophetic *hour of performance*, in the *time of manifestation* and in your *day of demonstration*. Heaven has called you and Earth cannot stop you!

You are not subject to Earth's economy and you are not limited by lack or by the circumstances that surround you. You will *not* go as far as you can take yourself, for the Spirit of God, *Himself,* is carrying you into new realms. You are on your way to the place that you never dreamed possible.

You are anointed by God for *this time*.
You are living in the *hour of power*.
You are the generation that is *called by Heaven*.
You are the redeemed *heirs of God*.

You have not only been visited by the anointing,
but you have become the HOUSE OF THE ANOINTING.

You are not only living in visitation,
but you have become THE HABITATION.

You are not just in revival,
but you are in RESTORATION.

3

PRINCIPLE 3
Specific Direction

Elijah told the widow woman to do whatever was necessary to fetch him some water. At his command, her spirit leapt within her! She recognized prophetic fulfillment. Turning aside, she served the man of God.

When the woman was *activated* for a mission, she was *interrupted*.

You have been activated, but you are getting interrupted in your activation because there is more for you than just fetching water. There is more for you than just what is necessary. There is more for your life than what you realize. There is provision for your purpose. There is superabundance for your life. There is an all-encompassing blessing coming to your house. That blessing will permanently change the caliber and quality of your living.

> **And as she was going to fetch it, he called to her, and said, "Bring me, I pray thee, a morsel of bread in thine hand."**
>
> **1 Kings 17:11**

The woman turned. Having been activated, she was on her way to do whatever was necessary to get water in a vessel. In the middle of her activation for a mission, she was interrupted. *"Bring me, I pray thee, a morsel of bread in thine hand,"* instructed the prophet.

As the woman walked away, Elijah recognized that *this* was the woman that had been commanded to sustain him. Immediately, he called out, *"Bring me in your hand a morsel of bread."* It's *specific direction*. Not only are you activated for a mission, but you are going to be given specific direction.

You are not a *"Generation of Whatever."* You are not a *"Person of Whatever."* You are not generic, for you have been given a *specific* call. **God has given you a specific commission, A MANDATE FOR YOUR LIFE.**

Now, at this hour of activation, He is going to give you *specific direction*.

"Bring me in your hand."

Why the specific direction, Elijah?
Why do I have to bring it in *my* hand?

"This is because I want YOU touching it. I want you as the point of contact that will enable my God – the One who has given me my name, Elijah (Jehovah is God). I want my God to see the SPECIFIC OBEDIENCE in your life and bring to you the economy that I am living under."

> You have been **activated for a mission**
>   interrupted with a **specific direction** and
>   included in a **divine economy**.

> GOD IS INTERRUPTING WHAT IS DEPLETING IN YOUR LIFE.
> THERE WILL BE NO *RUNNING OUT* IN YOUR LIFE.
> THERE WILL ONLY BE THE SOUND OF ABUNDANCE.

Specific direction: *"Bring me in thy hand a morsel of bread."*

This is where the woman hesitated. *Why?* She had been appointed by God to sustain the anointed, but time had passed and the land had become dry and unyielding. She went from a woman that had natural ability to sustain to a woman that had no natural ability to sustain.

God said, *"That is when I am going to show you My supernatural ability to sustain."*

And she said, "As the Lord thy God liveth, I have not a cake, but an handful of meal in a barrel, and a little oil in a cruse, and behold I am gathering two sticks, that I may go in and dress it for me and my son, that we may eat it, and die." And Elijah said unto her, "Fear not; go and do as thou hast said, but make thereof a little cake first, and bring it unto me, and after make for thee and thy son. For thus saith the Lord God of Israel, the barrel of meal shall not waste, neither shall the cruse of oil fail, until the day that the Lord sendeth rain upon the earth.'"

1 Kings 17:12-14

"Bring me in thy hand a morsel of bread." All she had was a handful.

The prophet caught her at the right time.

God has caught YOU at the right time.
He has caught you at the right hour.

Perilous times, darkness all over the world, violence, dead churches, unbelief, doctrines of devils, humanistic philosophies, and incurable diseases. There are all kinds of reasons to give in to fear, but God has caught you at the right time! He has activated you and given you a specific direction. He has interrupted you permanently. He has interrupted the thing that depletes in your life. *Now*, He will sustain you. *Now*, you will step into His supernatural abundance. This is the Word of the Lord for you *Now*.

God has included you in on a divine economy of all-inclusive abundance. He has inducted you into the supernatural climate of Heaven's economy. You have been embraced by Heaven's doings - by His demonstrations and manifestations.

Jesus said it like this, *"Seek ye first the Kingdom of God and His righteousness, and **all of these things** shall be added unto you"* (Matthew 6:33).

Specific Obedience

> And as she was going to fetch it, he called to her, and said, "Bring me, I pray thee, a morsel of bread in thine hand."
>
> 1 Kings 17:11

This woman had a choice. She could have said, *"You should have come three months ago. You are too late. All I have is a handful."* He said, *"I know what you have. That is why I said 'bring it in your hand.' I know what you are trying to do. You are going to cook your last. You have already reached the end but I have come to tell you that there is a new beginning that is coming to your life. There is a place of abundance in God. I have been sent to tell you that you are going to see a God that is not moved by the Earth's climate, but He is moving in your life to take care of every area of need. He is an all-inclusive God."*

Until prosperity hits the natural climate, **you are going to live in the realm of God's prosperity.**

Until all natural things are working together for good for you, **God is going to cause the invisible realm to take care of you.**

There is a dimension where Heaven has not only activated you, but specific direction has carried you into God's provision of abundance. It is a dimension where there is no longer a depleting force in your life. It is a realm where the creative power of abundant supply operates freely.

The first words out of Elijah's mouth were, *"Fear not. Go and do as you said, but make me a little cake first."*

Why would God send the woman home to go cook and to do whatever is necessary? Why would God have her make a cake for the anointed first - before he even steps foot into her house?

SPECIFIC DIRECTION...
necessitates SPECIFIC OBEDIENCE.

Before God gives your house *the fullness of His house,* He has to qualify your house as a place where He can be at home in. That qualification takes place through obedience – specific obedience. He said, *"You go ahead and obey this one thing and bring me a cake first."*

That was not going to be the last cake he ate!

4

PRINCIPLE 4
Corporate Supply

And she went and did according to the saying of Elijah, and she and he, and her house did eat many days. And the barrel of meal wasted not, neither did the cruse of oil fail, according to the word of the Lord, which he spake to Elijah.

1 Kings 17:15-16

She and her household ate for many days and many years because of her obedience. The Word of God states *"And she went and did according to the saying of Elijah..."* In other words, she received the word from the prophet and obeyed it. Her obedience yielded a great return.

Corporate Blessing.
Corporate Supply.

Her entire household ate. She was *activated, interrupted* and given *specific direction.* That specific direction took her from just knowing her mission to experiencing her *supernatural place of provision.* She entered into God's economy of abundance. As she obeyed the divine directive that was delivered to her, she received the faith necessary to step into an *experiential understanding of the prophet's reward.* Within that reward, was a corporate blessing for her house. She ate, Elijah ate and her whole house ate.

Corporate Supply.

Elijah ended up living at her house. It was a place of supply.

I Hear the Sound of Abundance

You may think that only three people – the widow, the son and Elijah – ate at that house. The Bible, however, does not say that three people ate. The Bible clearly states that she ate, Elijah ate *and the house ate*. There was no lack at *that* house. If she had cousins and relatives, they ate. If she had visitors, they ate too. There was corporate supply. Everyone was full. It was a place of abundance during famine.

Wherever the anointing dwells, there is an absence of lack.
Wherever the anointing resides, there is superabundance.

When Jesus sent Peter to get money out of the mouth of a fish, did it pay for two people's taxes?

When Jesus fed a multitude, did everyone eat?

Were there leftovers or was it just enough to get by?

Whenever Jesus multiplied food and fed a multitude, *they ate*. There is not one place in the Bible that says that Jesus just barely had enough to get by. *No*, the people ate until they were full. There were leftovers in abundance. It was an inexhaustible supply.

When Elijah said that the barrel of meal would not fail, he never put a limit on how many cakes she could cook everyday. He said, *"In your house nothing will deplete!"*

The widow woman had a barrel and a cruise that would not deplete. *Why?* She had a houseguest. There was a prophet that was called to live in the high chamber of a loft in her house. God made her a child of substance and saw to it that while the Earth was depleting, and while there was a terrible famine, she would have *a personal visitation of revival*. The anointing inhabited her house and her house became a feeding center, *a place of corporate supply*. In the middle of lack, she experienced a different economy.

It was a miracle barrel!

It was not *how much* she got in the barrel, but *Who* was in the barrel. When the prophet said, *"It will not waste or fail,"* he never placed a limit on how many times she could tap into that place of supply. Everyday her house had a miracle barrel of meal and miracle cruise of oil. It never failed. What started out as a handful, never failed to supply. It never wasted. Every time the widow took a handful out, *there was always a handful left*. When a handful didn't fill her, she would take out *another* handful. When that handful did not fill her, *there was still another handful left!* When her son ate a handful, *there was always a handful left!* When the prophet ate a few handfuls, *there was always a handful left*. There was abundance in that house!

Corporate Supply.

How long is she going to have the handful at her fingertips? She will have access to the supernatural supply for as long as there is a need for it. The day that the rains come and water the Earth will be the day that she will no longer need the miracle barrel.

Every morning she got up and went to make breakfast. The first handful she took out was for the anointed and the anointing. The second handful she took out was for her *and her house*. At noon, the first handful was for the anointed and the anointing. The second handful was for her *and her house*. When the sun had set, the first handful went to the anointing and the anointed. She then fed herself *and her house*. God gave her a principle that never failed in her life. Her activation and her obedience yielded the supernatural provision of God's corporate blessing. Everybody that came into that house walked into the economy of Almighty God. At that house, things multiplied. At that house, there was abundance for every day of the week.

It's the economy of God.

Fear Not, *Go* and *Do*

> And Elijah said unto her, "Fear not; go and do as thou hast said, but make thereof a little cake first, and bring it unto me, and after make for thee and thy son. For thus saith the Lord God of Israel, 'the barrel of meal shall not waste, neither shall the cruse of oil fail, until the day that the Lord sendeth rain upon the earth.'" And she went and did according to the saying of Elijah, and she and he, and her house did eat many days. And the barrel of meal wasted not, neither did the cruse of oil fail, according to the word of the Lord, which he spake to Elijah.
>
> 1 Kings 17:13-16

- **God sends a Word.**
- The Word proclaims, **"It's a done deal!"**
- An **internal activation** takes place.
- A **mission** is realized.
- Suddenly, God **interrupts**.
- It's the clear sound of **specific direction** for the mission.
- Specific direction necessitates **specific obedience**.
- Obedience gives way to the economy of **corporate supply**.
- Corporate Supply is a supernatural **Demonstration**.
- It's evidence of a **never exhaustible supply.**

As you obey the specific direction that God has already given you, corporate supply will overtake your life. You will cease to experience decrease. That which had been subject to natural depletion will replenish supernaturally. You will become a supplier. Your life will become a target for abundance and your whole household will dwell under Heaven's economy.

The account of Elijah and the widow woman is a type of *today's end-time generation*. **You are *that* generation!**

**God is working to bring YOUR LIFE
into His plan of
DEMONSTRATION AND MANIFESTATION.**

God is going to show off in your life.

My speech and my preaching was with demonstration of the Spirit and of power.

1 Corinthians 2:4

God will **accredit** His Word.
God will **prove** His Word.
God will **demonstrate** His Word.

Demonstration and **Manifestation**

He is a God of performance.
What was dormant is activated.
Purpose is re-ignited.
Your victory is a done deal.

Within His Word to you, there is an interruption that gives specific direction. It is not an easy direction. It is not a course without obstacles, but it will challenge you. It will call to your purpose. It will move you to walk, talk, live and breathe in Heaven's realm. You will say, *"My God. Wait a minute; THAT is all I have! You are asking me to step out on a limb."*

And Elijah said unto her, "FEAR NOT; *go* and *do*..."

1 Kings 17:13a

Before Elijah said anything, he said, *"Fear not!"* Specific direction from God will scare you. It is not a *human direction* that only requires natural ability. It is a *divine direction* that necessitates supernatural ability. It requires the boldness and confidence of FAITH founded IN THE SECURITY OF GOD'S WORD.

Stepping out of the boat to walk on water is not something that can be practiced. You do not learn it in kindergarten or in high school. It's not even taught in college or at the most prestigious medical schools. Most churches do not even touch on it! However, when the Word of God comes to you and says, *"Come!"* it will give you the **boldness and the ability** to step out of the boat and to walk.

The same word that gives you specific direction says, *"Fear not!"*

The specific obedience of the widow woman moved her out of the boat and into an economy of supernatural supply. Obedience ushered her into superabundance. There was not a day that she went hungry or an instance where her household went without. The meal did not fail. The oil did not run out. There was feast, not famine. Her connection with the prophetic anointing took the limits off of her life. It was the reward of the prophet in operation.

5

PRINCIPLE 5
The All-Inclusive Anointing

> And it came to pass after these things, that the son of the woman, the mistress of the house, fell sick, and his sickness was so sore, that there was no breath left in him. And she said unto Elijah, "What have I to do with thee, O thou man of God? Art thou come unto me and to call my sin to remembrance, and to slay my son?" And he said unto her, "Give me thy son." And he took him out of her bosom, and carried him up into a loft, where he abode, and laid him upon his own bed.
>
> 1 Kings 17:17-19

The boy died. The woman lamented to the prophet, *"What have I to do with thee, O thou man of God? Art thou come unto me and to call my sin to remembrance, and to slay my son?"* Perhaps this woman wasn't the purest woman on the planet. Chances are, she had issues. She made mistakes. She had a history. Like you, she was human and lived on planet Earth.

The prophet had a chamber in the loft of the woman's house. This was the same house that was under the economy of Heaven. This was the house of corporate supply. It was a house of supernatural abundance, yet her son *"fell sick, and his sickness was so sore, that there was no breath left in him."*

Corporate supply was available to supply for this situation. The woman, however, thought that it was only applicable to the miracle of food supply. She did not understand that **the supply of Heaven is comprehensive.** She did not understand that the prophet's reward was all-inclusive, that it was not limited to replenishing food. The power that resided in her home was there to do exceedingly abundantly above all that she could ask or think. Yet, her eyes were so full of the sheer magnitude of the problem, that she was unable to fathom the extent of the provision given her. The woman said in her mind, *"Yes, everything is great. My food supply does not deplete. We are sustained. God is obviously with this prophet, yet he is staying in MY house and I'm so unworthy..."*

Fear crept in. In the very back of her mind, she rehearsed her unworthiness. She meditated on the sins of her past and what she was deserving of. Consequently, sin bound her to fear and the widow found herself wondering what might go wrong next. This nagging fear opened the door to the enemy. It was an access point for him to do what he had no right to do. It opened the door to the Devourer. She did not know to close the door for she thought that only the Feeder lived in her loft. She didn't know that He was also the Resurrector, the Protector, the Deliverer, the Sustainer, the Provider and the Defender. His presence brought an all-inclusive anointing.

Our God is a lofty God! If He occupies the high place in your life, then do not make the mistake of thinking that it is just for the purpose of providing bread and water. There is an all-inclusive anointing in your life!

Job said, *"The thing that I greatly feared has come upon me"* (Job 3:25).

> BEFORE YOU FINISH THIS CHAPTER,
> AN ALL-POWERFUL COMMISSION
> WILL IGNITE YOU WITH SUPERNATURAL ABILITY TO MOW DOWN
> THOSE THINGS THAT HAVE THREATENED YOU.
> YOU WILL NOT TOLERATE ANY KIND OF EVIL IN YOUR LIFE!

DELIVERANCE AND REVIVAL!

The Threshold of Breakthrough

> And he cried unto the Lord, and said, "O Lord my God, hast thou also brought evil upon the widow whom I sojourn, by slaying her son?" And he stretched himself upon the child three times, and cried out unto the Lord, and said, "O Lord my God, I pray Thee, let the child's soul comes into him again." And the Lord heard the voice of Elijah; and the soul of the child came into him again, and he revived. And Elijah took the child, and brought him down out of the chamber into the house, and delivered him unto his mother; and Elijah said, "See, thy son liveth." And the woman said to Elijah, "Now by this I know that thou art a man of God, and that the Word of the Lord in thy mouth is the truth."
>
> 1 Kings 17:20-24

The woman knew that this was a man of God. She would not have given him the upper chamber of their home if she had not been convinced of this. Her confession in verse twenty-four proves it. She knew he was a man of God; the enemy however, had sown seeds of fear, doubt and unbelief in her heart.

The woman did not have a problem with supernatural supply. She knew that the food would replenish itself as long as she continued to scoop up the meal, bake the cake, and feed the man of God. She understood the supernatural mechanics of this miracle, but she continued to allow fear to meddle in the soil of her life. She allowed this fear because she did not understand **the all-inclusive nature of corporate supply**.

Your adversary, the devil, will always remind you of your history – of the sins and failures in your past. God has already taken care of these things, but if you are not diligent to cast these imaginations down, fear will creep into your heart. As fear festers, you will begin to wonder what will go wrong next. Eventually, unchecked fear-based meditations will produce after its kind.

In the back of this woman's mind, she was fearful that something was about to go terribly wrong. It had occurred to her that perhaps Elijah had come to her house to punish her for her sins. She was mindful of her past. When a person is mindful of their sins, they will always fear the worst.

Faith is an absolute assurance of the outcome.
Fear is the opposite.

Faith expects what God promises to come to pass.
Fear wonders what might go wrong.

The anointing was in the loft. The blessing was in the cake. The multiplication was in the oil. The power was in the house. The woman, however, could not implement this all-inclusive blessing because fear was dominating her life. She was at the threshold of her breakthrough, but paralyzed to enter into it because of fear and doubt.

The first thing she said was what she had been meditating on: *"Things are great. This food will never run out. My household will always eat. But I've got righteousness in the upper chamber. I have the anointing in the upper chamber and I have sins in my past."*

She feared what God had sent to be a blessing in her life.
She meditated on it.
She thought about it.
She talked about it.
It became bigger than life.

Fear will preach to you.
It will whisper, *"You are going to get what you deserve."*

The Word will preach to you too.

It will proclaim, *"What you are going to get is what Jesus procured for you."*

> **"What have I to do with thee, O thou man of God? Art thou come unto me and to call my sin to remembrance, and to slay my son?"**
>
> **1 Kings 17:18**

God did not kill her son. There are certain areas of judgment in the Bible, but this was not one of them. In this account, the widow's fear-based meditations gave access to a spirit of death. After losing her husband, she had mentally rehearsed the death of her beloved son. She had contemplated it, feared it and shuddered at the thought. That spirit came into her house through her confession and brought the curse she had been meditating on.

God did not send this prophet to the widow's house because her perfection qualified her for a visitation.

God looked for a widow that would:

HEAR the Word
Receive it as a DONE DEAL,
Receive ACTIVATION,
Receive SPECIFIC DIRECTION, and
OBEY the Word.

The first thing that the prophet said to the woman was, ***"FEAR NOT!"*** The woman thought that the prophet was just talking about food. She did not comprehend that the "Fear Not" reached into every area of her life. It was all-inclusive.

When fear had produced its fruit and the child had died, she brought his body to the prophet. He took the child, put him on his own bed and called on his Living God. The prophet laid himself on the child, released life into him and brought him back to life.

Her son was revived.
The widow *believed*.
She was instantly *delivered* of doubt.

When the Word says, *"Fear not!"* there is nothing to fear. When the anointing is in the house, there is **abundance, all-inclusive blessing** and **corporate supply**. God's blessings are inexhaustible.

The Prophet's Reward

There are some things that have short-circuited your results. You thought that you were unworthy, but God has sent THIS WORD to you today. Like the widow, this is your hour of appointment. This is your time of deliverance and revival. **This is the prophet's reward for your life.** It is all-inclusive in nature and its abundance will reach into every facet of your life to bring *God's best*.

God is destroying the power of fear in your life. What has been short-circuited is being resurrected. Always remember, there is nothing to fear because the One living in your house is committed to taking care of your house. He has an invested interest in your success, your promotion and your increase. You are not on your way down; you are on your way up! You are living in the hour of fulfillment.

Therefore, do not tolerate ONE MOMENT of fear in your life! Cast down those things that threaten your destiny. Do not give place to the devil, but resist him and he will flee.

God has made provision for your life. He has situated you beautifully, like a brilliant city on a hill, in the midst of superabundance. Your light will so shine before men. Your testimony will be seen by all and all will know that your God is Jehovah.

He is going to **pay your bills.**
He is going to **supply your superabundance.**
He is going to **cancel your debts.**
He is going to **heal your body.**
He is going to **save your lost loved ones.**
He is going to **build your home.**
He is going to **establish your walk.**

He is going to **direct your life.**
He is going to **impact you.**

My God has sent the anointing into your life because **you are the house of God.** You are the habitation of God through the Spirit. You are God's heritage. You are God's handiwork.

The thing that was short-circuited, the thing that was delayed, the thing that had become lame, is now being brought down from the lofty place. It is coming from the place of His headship in your life. Like the resurrected child, it is being brought down into your lap. *Fear not,* this is the prophet's reward.

It is an all-inclusive abundance.

It is happening right now.

Prophetic Declarations

Thus saith the Lord:

I will **demonstrate.**
I will **accredit.**
I will **witness.**
I will **perform.**

> This is the hour
> when I will go **ABOVE AND BEYOND**
> even the greatest expectations of my children.

I will make a DISTINCTION
by the power of My arm
between those who dwell
in the realm of the anointing
and those who back off of the power of My Word's light.

I will make a distinction with your life
and cause your lives to witness from on high…

>…from a realm of **promotion,**
>>…from a realm of **influence,**
>>>…from a realm of **gratitude,**
>>>>…from a realm of **gratification**.

There will be an **all-inclusive demonstration**
of MY NEVER-FAILING POWER.

There will not be a snare that will be tolerated
or a yoke that will continue to have strength.

There will not be a burden that will steal the song,
or a heavy weight that will take away the sound.

There will not be a shame that will bow the head,
or a sorrow of things gone by.

There will be a hope with reference to
the immediacy of My mighty power

and faith in reference to
the presence of My holiness.

I WILL...
Cure the incurable.
Perform the impossible.
Eliminate the aggravating.
Impart the activating.

You will rise up to witness,
not only when you open your mouth,
but *your life will be a sermon that speaks...*
...day in and day out.

I will be in the midst of you as
A GOD OF SUPERABUNDANCE.

**The ALL-INCLUSIVE ANOINTING
will be seen in your life.**

Nations will recognize...
...that My Name is in the midst of you.

> It is a Name of a **NOW PERFORMANCE.**
> It is a Name of a **NOW ACTIVITY.**
> It is a Name of a **NOW VICTORY.**

My Word for you is a Word of Yea and Amen.

So rejoice and be glad,
for that which YOU do not understand,

and that which YOU cannot make happen,
and that which YOU do not know how to do,
I WILL NOW PERFORM before your very eyes.

For what your heart will expect…
will be *exceeded by My Word,*
EXCEEDINGLY ABUNDANTLY
above all that you can ask or think.

I AM PREPARING YOU for what you
have not been prepared for
because what is about to happen,
you are not prepared for.
It will shock you…
…even as I have prepared you.

I will prepare you to recognize that it is of Me.
But, I do not prepare you to *comprehend* and *contain*…
the vastness of its magnitude
BECAUSE IT IS BIGGER
than you could ever think or imagine.

It is the Lord

What was declared to you prophetically is happening to you and to multiplied-millions around the Earth. What I just prophesied over your life through the pages of this book is happening right now. Even as you read this, God is preparing you for something that will shock you *anyway*. He is preparing, training and equipping you through the power of His Word.

When God performs and demonstrates His Word with evidence, you will not say, *"Oh, I have seen that before."* No, you are a part of a generation that is called to inherit what no other generation has ever seen! You will only be prepared to say, *"It is the Lord."*

It is important that you understand *what* the Lord has just released prophetically into the atmosphere of your life. *"According to my word, it is a done deal."* When it is released, it does not return void. When it is released, it goes to work. When it is released, you and I have a responsibility to pray it.

You have a right to claim what was released. God said prophetically, *"I am going to stretch My hand. I am going to perform. I am going to demonstrate in your life so that you, in the now, will experience a demonstration of evidence that God's Word is so. You will also experience a transformation and a change that is bigger than your expectation. It is beyond what you are prepared for. You are only going to be able to recognize it is of God. You will not be able to say, 'I have had that before. I have seen that before. It is no big deal.'"*

The Hundredfold Principle

> And he entered into one of the ships, which was Simon's (Peter's), and prayed him that he would thrust out a little from the land. And he sat down, and taught the people out of the ship. Now when he had left speaking, he said unto Simon, "Launch out into the deep, and let down your nets for a draught (catch)." And Simon answering said unto him, "Master, we have toiled all the night, nevertheless at thy word I will let down the net."
>
> Luke 5:3-5

Peter was a professional fisherman. Although he was a professional at his trade, he didn't have any fish. He had toiled all night and come up with nothing. In the morning, Peter allowed Jesus to use his boat. Jesus preached a Word to the multitude and then turned to the wearied fisherman. He instructed Peter, *"Launch out into the deep and throw your nets in for a catch."* Jesus, of course, was expecting more than what Peter was expecting! Peter replied, *"We have toiled all night and caught nothing. Nevertheless at Thy word..."*

It was a done deal.

> And when they had this done, they inclosed a great multitude of fishes: and their net brake. And they beckoned unto their partners, which were in the other ship, that they should come and help them. And they came, and filled both the ships so that they began to sink.
>
> Luke 5:7

Peter threw in the net and caught such a great amount of fish that it terrified him. It was a miracle-catch! In fact, the catch was so great that it broke the net and almost sunk two boats! It was exceedingly abundantly above all that he could ask or think. It was bigger than anything he had ever seen. The supply was excessive. Astounded, the seasoned fisherman immediately dropped to his knees before Jesus. He said, *"Depart from me, O Lord, for I am a sinful man"* (Luke 5:8).

For he was astonished, and all that were with him, at the draught of the fishes which they had taken.

Luke 5:9

Peter was prepared to meet Christ, but he was not prepared for the kind of results Christ was going to demonstrate. Peter was a professional, but in his entire professional career, he had never captured what he captured that day *"at Thy Word."*

The results astonished him to the point of fear. Peter was afraid that if there was such righteousness on his boat, that he might get the negative side of God's hand. Religion teaches you that God is going to give you a *backhand* when He is really offering you *His hand*.

And Jesus said unto Simon. *Fear not;* **from henceforth thou shalt catch men.**

Luke 5:10b

The day that Jesus stepped into Peter's boat was a day of appointment for Peter. He received a word that not only launched him into his ministry and commissioned him for his specific call, but it introduced him into the God-kind of economy. From that day forward, EVERY AREA of his life became a testimony of God's superabundance.

This account is one of many examples throughout the Bible that underscores the operation of **the hundredfold principle.**

The hundredfold principle is God's best for your life. It is a level of increase and promotion that finds its source within a realm of inexhaustible supply.

> Jesus answered and said, "Verily I say unto you, there is no man that hath left house, or brethren, or sisters, or father, or mother, or wife, or children, or lands, for my sake, and the gospel's, but *he shall receive an hundredfold now in this time,* houses and brethren, and sisters, and mothers, and children, and lands, with persecutions; and in the world to come eternal life."
>
> Mark 10:29-30

> ...They inclosed a great multitude of fishes: and their net break....and they...filled both the ships, so that they began to sink.
>
> Luke 5:6b,7b

> Jesus said, "...go thou to the sea, and cast an hook, and take up the fish that first cometh up: and when thou has opened his mouth, thou shalt find a piece of money; that take, and give unto them for me and thee."
>
> Matthew 17:27b

> They cast therefore, and now they were not able to draw it for the multitude of fishes.
>
> John 21:6b

> And they did all eat, and were filled. And they took up twelve baskets full of the fragments and the fishes.
>
> Mark 6:42-43

Neither was there any among them that lacked..."

Acts 4:34a

A multitude was fed, many fish were caught, taxes were paid and none among them lacked. These accounts demonstrate God's willingness to pour the fullness of His abundance into your life. God's best in your day-to-day walk is exceedingly abundantly above all that you could think or ask. His perfect will for you, *one hundred percent* of the time, is *one hundredfold*.

Ever-Increasing Abundance

God has been preparing you. He has prepared you and He will keep on preparing you. What He is doing, however, *you are not prepared for.*

By virtue of human nature, we have been taught to go by what we see. We need the evidence and the confirmation of those who will continually speak to us about what is taking place beyond our natural vision. God has no limits. His ability is not measured with the ability of mankind. The *only* limits He has are the ones that *you* put on Him in your own mind. Your concept of his willingness to provide is the only thing that is slowing you down. That is precisely why God wants you to take the limits off.

**Allow yourself to be prepared
for the performance of an unlimited God.**

You will only be prepared to recognize *"It is the Lord."* For when it happens, it will still astonish you, yet it will bear witness within you. God will show off in your life. He will accredit Himself. He will perform. He will validate that His Word is true. He will show that His will is an active Word. Even in the arena of your profession, the Lord will show off in your life. Like Peter, you will be astonished for your experience will exceed the results that you are accustomed to.

Now unto Him that is able to do exceedingly abundantly above all that we ask or think, according to the power that worketh in us.

Ephesians 3:20

The Lord is able to do **ACCORDING TO the resident power** that works *in you.* The resident power is the indwelling of Christ.

He lives in you and moves through you. It is His power that is actively working in you.

You are getting stirred by the power of His Word to the point of *superabundant, divine, expectation.*

The immediate PERFORMANCE will astonish you. You will see results that you have never seen. Your experience will exceed your expectations. This is the hour of superabundance. *Limit not the Holy One of Israel in your midst* (Psalm 78:4). His power is with you to perform.

Take the limits off of Almighty God in your life!

He is Omnipotent. He is *all-powerful.*
He is Omniscient. He is *all-knowing.*
He is Omnipresent. He is *all-present.*

Take the limits off of Him!
He is not limited to a geographical *location*
because He is everywhere.

Take the limits off of Him!
He is not limited by your *understanding*
because He knows everything.

Take the limits off of Him!
He is not limited by your *ability*
because He is all-powerful.

Allow God to perform in your life
BEYOND ANYTHING that you have ever seen
or are capable of procuring or performing
in your own ability.

It is according to the resident power in you
that HE IS GOING TO DO ABOVE AND BEYOND
what you can think or imagine.

There is power in you. It is a power that performs. It is a power that transforms. It is a power that is inexhaustible. That power is working in you, day and night, to do exceedingly abundantly above all that you could ask, think or imagine.

Your inheritance is greater than your revelation!

Unlimited Invitation

What gives God **UNLIMITED INVITATION** in your life to do these things?

Trust in the Lord with all thine heart and lean not unto thine own understanding.

Proverbs 3:5

Like Peter, you will say, *"In all of my years of fishing, I have never had a day like today."*

Like Joshua, *before you think*, you will speak to celestial bodies. You will stop the natural course of the universe in order to win the victory of today!

They will write about you. They will talk about you. *They will tell of the ones* that have taken the limits off of Almighty God.

You are trusting in *Someone* that cannot be hindered by the human intellect or by the limitation of man's inability. He is Almighty God. He is in you and there is resident power to perform! **Your unlimited invitation to the Lord, will release Him to usher you into the length and breadth of uncharted abundance.**

Those that know the Word, know that within it, *there is more to know that what they know.* So they continue to look into the Word. They continue to study it. As they do, it not only expands and enlarges their *knowledge of His ability*, but it also increases their *knowledge of their capacity to receive His performance.*

This day is like no other day in your entire Christian existence.

Unlimited Invitation

There has never been a day like today.

Supernatural Results

> Simon Peter saith unto them, "I go a fishing." They say unto him, "We also go with thee." They went forth, and entered into a ship immediately; and that night they caught nothing. But when the morning was now come, Jesus stood on the shore: but the disciples knew not that it was Jesus. The Jesus saith unto them, "Children have ye any meat?" They answered him, "No." And he said unto them, "Cast the net on the right side of the ship, and ye shall find."
>
> John 21:3-6a

Jesus had risen from the dead, but the disciples had not yet received the Baptism of the Holy Ghost. Not knowing quite what to do with themselves, Peter announced to the others, *"I go a fishing."* The other disciples replied, *"We also go with thee."* They boarded a boat and toiled all night. They exhausted their natural ability, but caught nothing. When morning had come, a man called out to them from the shore.

> **Children, have ye any meat?**
>
> John 21:5b

The exhausted fishermen replied, *"No!"* Jesus, answering them, said, *"Cast your net in on the right side of the ship and you shall find."* Obedient to His Word, they threw the net in and caught something that exceeded all natural probabilities.

> **They cast therefore, and now they were not able to draw it for the** *multitude of fish.*
>
> John 21:6b

Immediately recognizing the supernatural results, they said, *"It is the Lord!"* They recognized *Who it was by the results.* It was a catch that was beyond their natural ability. It was abundance that exceeded natural probabilities. Only the supernatural power of God could produce such a great manifestation and demonstration of supply.

> HIS RESULTS WILL ASTONISH YOU.
> IF IT IS ACCORDING TO HIS WORD, IT IS A DONE DEAL.

Peter immediately leaped out of the boat, plunged into the water and swam towards Jesus on the shore! He was overwhelmed at the revival, the visitation, the provision, and the resurrection in God's results. When he got to the shore, *Jesus already had a feast prepared for them.* There's always superabundance for God's people. He will do exceedingly abundantly above all that you could ask or think.

Prepare yourself for what you are not ready for!

When God does something for you,
it is not *exactly* what you want,
because it is **EXCEEDING ABUNDANTLY ABOVE**
all that you could <u>ever want.</u>

God's Best

> Now a certain man was sick, named Lazarus, of Bethany, the town of Mary and her sister Martha.
>
> John 11:1

Lazarus became sick and was close to death. His sisters, Mary and Martha, sent urgent word to Jesus. They wanted a healing for their brother. Despite their best efforts, Lazarus died and was buried. Jesus arrived on the fourth day. Everyone thought the Lord was too late.

> **And many of the Jews came to Martha and Mary to comfort them concerning their brother. Then Martha, as soon as she heard that Jesus was coming, went and met him...Then said Martha unto Jesus, "Lord, if thou hadst been there, my brother had not died."**
>
> **John 11:19-20a, 21**

If Lazarus had been healed before his death, that house would have had a healing testimony. They were ready for that healing, but when he died, things began to look bleak. If Lazarus had been resurrected on the *first day*, they would have had a testimony that their brother was raised on the first day. If Jesus had raised him on the *second day*, they would have had a second day testimony of resurrection. Even if Jesus had raised him on the *third day*, they would have had a third day testimony of resurrection. *On the fourth day, however, a resurrection seemed impossible.* Nobody was expecting a miracle of this caliber. His body had begun to decompose and all hope was seemingly lost.

> **Jesus said, "Take away the stone. Martha, the sister of him that was dead, saith unto him, "Lord, by this time**

he stinketh: for he hath been dead four days."

John 11:39

When Jesus arrived, they were prepared to see Jesus, but they were not prepared for what Jesus could do. They knew He could heal. They might have known that He could raise the dead, however, no one imagined that He could raise someone who had been decomposing for four days. *They did not understand the nature of the all-inclusive blessing.*

Lazarus is buried. The body is decomposing. The sisters are in mourning. Here comes Jesus and His entourage of disciples. He says, *"I did not come to do just what you are expecting. I came to do BEYOND WHAT YOU ARE EXPECTING, because the testimony I am going to give you, is going to be greater than any generation has ever had!"*

Jesus saith unto her, "Said I not unto thee, that, if though wouldest believe, thou shouldest see the glory of God?

John 11:40

When you believe, you will see that which you were not expecting. You will see what you have never seen before. It is all-inclusive. The blessing cannot be exhausted or depleted. God does not ration His power to His children. There is abundant provision and supernatural supply for every situation. That abundance is ever increasing to produce God's best in your life.

I am not teaching you that you cannot have what you are believing for. You can, but I am telling you that *the lesser is included in the greater.* **When the greater performs, not only is your *lesser* met, but the *greater* is also performed in your life.** This is the nature of the all-inclusive blessing. It is God's best for you today.

Testifying to Your Destiny

> He (Jesus) cried with a loud voice, "Lazarus, come forth." And he that was dead came forth...
>
> **John 11:43b-44a**

Before raising Lazarus, Jesus had said, *"This sickness is not unto death but for the glory of God that the Son of Man will be glorified thereby"* (John 11:4b).

When Jesus confessed this, it was a done deal. It did not matter after that. It did not matter what anyone said or how insurmountable the obstacle seemed. Jesus was coming with a word that was loaded with the supernatural, reviving, delivering, and restoring power of Almighty God.

He raised Lazarus from the dead and restored his physical body. He gave Lazarus a testimony that no man in human history had.

> YOU ARE A CHILD OF DESTINY.
> YOU HAVE YOUR OWN CALL, YOUR OWN VISITATION, YOUR OWN TESTIMONY, AND YOUR OWN APPOINTMENT.
> YOUR MINISTRY AND CALL IS NOT A REPETITION.
> IT IS NOT A REPLICA OR A REDUNDANCY IN GOD.

There is a uniqueness to your testimony.

God has made an **ORIGINAL** out of you.

The Bible records that they sent a note to Jesus saying, *"The one that you love is sick"* (John 11:3). Jesus took the one that He loved and gave him a testimony that nobody in history had ever had. From Adam until Lazarus, nobody could say, *"I was in the*

Dr. John Avanzini ministering on the set of Miracles Today.

Dr. Robin & Dr. Christian Harfouche with Dr. Morris Cerullo.

Dr. Harfouche returning with Dr. Morris Cerullo from an awesome series of meetings in Latin America.

Dr. Robin & Dr. Christian Harfouche with Dr. Lester Sumrall.

Dr. Christian Harfouche with Dr. Norvel Hayes.

School of Acts in Malaysia.

City Harvest Church in Singapore.

Mass crusades in Latin America.

"Victory."

The sick are ministered to in Latin America.

Dr. Harfouche on the set of Miracles Today.

Dr. Christian & Dr. Robin Harfouche
ministering in the prophetic.

The sick are healed during New England Miracle Crusades.

Dr. Christian & Dr. Robin while ministering in Africa.

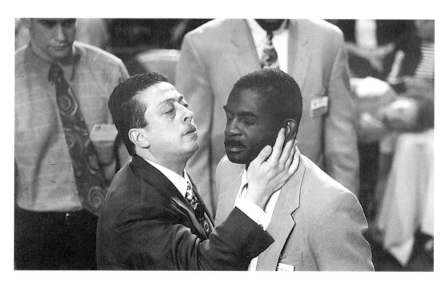

The deaf hear at a campmeeting in Tampa, Florida.

Filming an interview segment of the Miracles Today show.

Dr. Robin asking Dr. Christian questions during the closing portion of the show.

Altar Call in Kuala Lumpur, Malaysia.

Dr. Harfouche ministering in Malaysia.

Thousands ministered to in Indonesia.

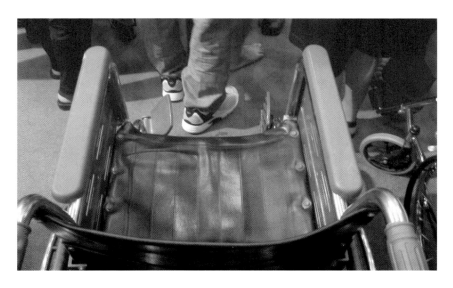

The wheelchairs were emptied in Indonesia.

The sick are healed in Singapore.

School of Signs & Wonders, Italy.

Dr. Harfouche ministering during a School of Signs & Wonders in Italy.

Dr. Harfouche ministering with Reverend R.W. Schambach on the set of Miracles Today.

grave four days and God raised me up to go preach about revival."

Revival is an awakening and a resurrection. It's a restoration of what was decomposed, what was decayed, stolen, and marked as permanently lost. God put it all in one miracle. Lazarus was a walking testimony. Everywhere he put his feet, he testified to revival. God loved him so much that He gave him a testimony unlike anyone else.

God is going to give you **a miracle.**
God is going to give you **a gift.**
God is going to give you **an anointing.**
God is going to give you **a financial experience.**
God is going to give you **a supernatural visitation.**
God is going to give you **a divine calling.**

Nobody but Lazarus could have said, *"I was in the grave four days."*

I am *not* looking for what God has done for others so that I can tell Him to do it for me. I am *not* looking back and saying, *"Do it again, Lord."* I am only looking back to say, *"Do more!"*

God's Word is a NOW WORD.

Enoch and Elijah had wonderful testimonies. Elijah went up in a whirlwind and Enoch walked with God and God took him. They both left testimonies, but the testimony that Enoch had was before his translation.

For before his translation he had this testimony, that he pleased God.

Hebrews 11:5b

The translation was the testimony!
His catching away was his testimony!

**GOD IS PREPARING YOU AND HE
WILL CONTINUE TO PREPARE YOU
for what you are not prepared for.**

YOU are the Testimony!

And Jesus, when he came out, saw much people, and was moved with compassion toward them, because they were as sheep not having a shepherd: and he began to teach them many things. And when the day was far spent, his disciples came unto him, and said, "This is a desert place, and now the time is far passed..."

Mark 6:34-35

Jesus was preaching to the multitudes. They came from every town and every village to hear His Words. Towards the latter half of the day, the disciples came to Jesus with a concern. *"Send the people away to go buy food because they have nothing to eat"* (Mark 6:36). The people were hungry and evening was fast approaching.

Jesus was caught up in the Word! He knew that His Word was an all-inclusive Word. He knew that he could not talk about the abundance of Heaven and leave empty bellies. He couldn't talk about tomorrow and leave an empty today.

The anointing that you are under right now is an all-inclusive anointing.

Jesus answered His disciples and said, *"You feed them."*

The disciples had been prepared. They had seen many miracles during their time of training with Him. His word of instruction, however, shocked them. They were prepared, but they were not ready for the extravagant proportion of this miracle. They were only ready to identify that *"It is the Lord."*

> "There is a lad here, which hath five barley loaves, and two small fishes; but what are they among so many?"
>
> John 6:9

Upon hearing Jesus' challenge, one of the disciples mentions that there is a boy in the crowd with five barley loaves and two small fish. *"But what are they among so many?"* he asks. The supply in his hand was insufficient to meet such a great need. It was an impossibility, yet Jesus said, *"You feed them."* This disciple was not ready for this miracle, but he was about to see the God who is able to do exceedingly abundantly above all that he can ask or think (Ephesians 3:20).

Jesus took the lunch and blessed it.

We are blessed by God.

Whatever is blessed of God **multiplies.**
Whatever is blessed of God **is more than enough.**
Whatever is blessed of God **knows no limits.**
Whatever is blessed of God **will not stop.**

He took the lunch, looked up and blessed the food. He did not look at the disciples because their sermon was, *"But what are these among so many."*

> **And Jesus took the loaves; and when He had given thanks, He distributed to the disciples, and the disciples to them that were set down; and likewise of the fishes as much as they would. When they were filled, He said unto His disciples, "Gather up the fragments that remain, that nothing be lost." Therefore they gathered them together, and filled twelve baskets with the fragments of the five barley loaves, which remained over and above unto them that had eaten.**
>
> John 6:11-13

YOU are the Testimony!

After everyone had eaten and was full, Jesus instructed His disciples to *collect the leftovers*. They gathered *twelve baskets* of what was left over from the five barley loaves. In the natural, it was impossible. It was beyond anything that they could have imagined. It was exceedingly abundantly above all that they could ask or think.

Jesus gave the boy a testimony. Up until that day, there had never been a boy on the Earth whose little lunch fed a multitude. No boy could say, *"My lunch fed the multitude. I had to get helpers in order to carry the twelve baskets."*

> GOD HAS PREPARED YOU. GOD IS PREPARING YOU
> AND GOD WILL KEEP ON PREPARING YOU
> *FOR WHAT YOU ARE NOT PREPARED FOR.*
> ONCE YOU TRUST AND ACCEPT,
> GOD WILL MAKE *YOU* THE TESTIMONY.

**If you listen closely now,
you will *hear* the prophetic word of invitation.
You will hear and identify *the sound of abundance*
coming upon your life.**

YOU ARE THE TESTIMONY of God's all-inclusive blessing!

Going to the Other Side

> Now it came to pass on a certain day, that He went into a ship with His disciples: and He said unto them, "Let us go over unto the other side of the lake." And they launched forth.
>
> Luke 8:22

Jesus and His disciples boarded a ship to go to the other side. While in the ship, a storm came and began to beat on it. The wind was blowing violently and their vessel began to fill with water. At least one third of Jesus' disciples were seasoned fisherman. It takes a lot to scare people who are well acquainted with the waters! These disciples, however, were afraid and felt that their lives were in immediate peril. They were terrified because they forgot that **according to my word, it is a done deal**. Jesus said, *"Come let us go to the other side."*

> WHEN YOU WERE CALLED TO BE A CHRISTIAN, YOU WERE **CALLED TO THE OTHER SIDE**. JESUS DOES NOT CALL HIS PEOPLE TO THE SAME SIDE. HE CALLS HIS OWN TO THE OTHER SIDE.

There is no devil; there is no whim; there is no storm; there is no wave; there is no raging opposition that will stop us from the side that God has called us to! Your destination is awaiting you. Your destination is calling you. You have been called to this hour of prophetic destiny.

> Your DESTINATION and your DESTINY
> are tied right into your IDENTITY.

The ship filled with water, yet in the midst of the storm, Jesus continued to sleep. The disciples, however, were convinced that death was imminent.

> **...and there came down a storm of wind on the lake: and they were filled with water, and were in jeopardy.**
>
> **Luke 8:23b**

These were people that had been prepared, were presently being prepared, and that would continue to be prepared for what they were not prepared for.

> **Where unto I also labor, striving according to his working, which worketh in me mightily.**
>
> **Colossians 1:29**

> **...which is Christ in you, the hope of glory.**
>
> **Colossians 1:27**

The terrified disciples awoke Jesus. They cried out, *"Master, master, we perish"* (Luke 8:24)! Jesus arose, rebuked the storm and commanded the waters to be still. Immediately, there was a great calm. Upon seeing this supernatural demonstration, the disciples feared exceedingly. These were the same disciples that had seen it all. They had seen all of the miracles that He had performed. They had seen all of the Word that He had spoken come to pass, *but they had not seen this.*

> GOD IS PREPARING YOU FOR WHAT YOU ARE NOT PREPARED FOR. DO NOT STRUGGLE WITH IT, BUT BE PREPARED FOR THE THINGS *THAT YOU HAVE NEVER IMAGINED OR EXPECTED.*

Be prepared *for what people said would never happen in your life.*

Be prepared *for the things that will exceed your wildest imaginations.*

Be prepared *for the happenings of God to take place in your life now.*

Jesus calmed the storm. The same people that were afraid of dying, were afraid of this kind of man. Looking at each other, they said:

What manner of man is this! For He commandeth even the winds and water, and they obey him.

Luke 8:25b

Jesus did everything He did as a man anointed by the Holy Ghost. Therefore, He is the *manner of man* who has the God-Kind of faith. He knows that *whosoever shall say and not doubt in his heart, but shall believe, the things that he says shall come to pass* (Mark 11:23). He shall have whatsoever he says. That is the kind of man Jesus is. This is the kind of person that scares people! It is this kind of person that has no problem being prepared for what he or she has not been prepared for!

Show me any person that is mightily used by God in the Bible and I will show you a person performing things they have never performed before.

The disciples had no idea that when the storm came, the gift would arise. When Jesus arose, the storm had no chance.

You are filled with *God wind!* You are filled with the *breath of God!* Whatever comes against you, **the gift of God will rise up in you**. You will say, *"No, God's Word said we are going to the other side."*

God's Word says *we will never deplete!*
God's Word says *we will always increase!*
God's Word says *there are no limits!*
God's Word says *abundance is for today!*
God's Word says *it is for the now!*

Guarding Your Destiny

The widow woman experienced both deliverance and restoration.

And the woman said to Elijah, "Now by this I know that thou art a man of God, and that the Word of the Lord in thy mouth is the truth."

1 Kings 17:24

The woman knew that Elijah was a man of God. She believed the word of provision in the arena of the meal and the oil. It was not a problem to believe that they would continue to eat. However, there was something she set into motion with her own words.

The first time she met Elijah, she told him:

"As the Lord thy God liveth, I have not a cake, but an handful of meal in a barrel, and a little oil in a cruse, and behold I am gathering two sticks, *that I may go in and dress it for me and my son, that we may eat it, and die."*

1 Kings 17:12

Death was something she continually meditated upon. As her resources depleted and the famine wore on, she found herself mentally rehearsing the worst. In her mind, she saw the thing she greatly feared. Her fear was not starvation for herself, but that of her beloved son. She was afraid that he would die. During their first meeting at the city gate, the prophet said, *"Fear not!"* to the widow. He gave her *specific direction.*

Partnership with the anointing will drive decrease out of your house! In the middle of a region full of lack and famine, *there was a house full of supply.* It was a house where the anointing presided.

The woman got in on the miracle of supply but she never heeded the, *"Fear not!"* She never *"feared not"* death. The thing she feared the most came upon her son.

When Elijah told her, *"Fear not!"* he was giving her the answer to the thing that was trying to dominate her. He was giving her the answer that, if employed, would shut the door to the enemy.

If I regard iniquity in my heart, the Lord will not hear me.

Psalm 66:18

Thy Word have I hid in my heart, that I might not sin against thee.

Psalm 119:11

For whatsoever is not of faith, is sin.

Romans 14:23

Fear is not of faith. Fear is sin. This woman said, *"Did you come here to bring back to my remembrance my transgression?"* The only person that remembered her transgression was her! In the back of her mind, her greatest fear was that her transgressions would ultimately kill her son. She regarded her transgressions, but the Psalmist said *"If I regard iniquity in my heart, the Lord will not hear me"* (Psalm 66:18).

What should she have filled her heart with?

"Thy Word have I hid in my heart, that I might not sin against thee" (Psalm 119:11).

Her meditations and her confession should have been, *"Your Word in my heart is a done deal."*

Although the woman received a breakthrough in corporate food supply, she left an open door to the enemy. She didn't settle the *"Fear not!"* in her heart. As a result, she wasn't able to recognize that the **all-inclusive anointing** also supplied for her protection.

Your adversary is very legalistic in nature. If he can get you in an area where you distrust God, he will step in and take territory.

GUARD YOUR DESTINY with God's Word!

It's BIGGER than You!

Despite this open door, the widow woman was seeing daily performance. When her son did die, she did not only get a resurrection for her son, but she received an instantaneous deliverance from ever fearing God again. She was set free and received a powerful revelation. Her revelation was this: **In my mouth, there is an all-inclusive word. God does not bless me in one area and diminish me in another area.**

The woman got more than she expected!

When you accepted Christ as your savior, they told you that He was your ticket to Heaven. They just told you, *"You are saved. You will live forever."*

You already have the **Resurrection**.
You already have the **Life**.
You already have the **Provider**.
You already have the **Healer**.
You already have the **Protector**.
You already have the **Preserver**.
You already have the **wisdom of God**.
You already have the **mind of Christ**.
You already have **more than you expected**.

You are discovering WHAT you have,
but YOU CANNOT CONTAIN ALL THAT YOU HAVE,
because your vessel is not big enough to wrap itself around
ALL that God has given you.

This is why the Word of God does not only say, *"Christ is in you!"* but it also says, *"You are in Christ."*

You do not only have Him in you. You are in Him. This is

because **you have Someone that is bigger than your container**. You have more blessings than you can house. Christ is an ocean. You are baptized into Christ. He is not only in you flowing like rivers of living water, but you are also in Him. He is not only in you springing up as a well of salvation unto eternal life, but you are also in Him.

She received more than resurrection.
She received DELIVERANCE.

She received more than deliverance.
She received RESTORATION.

She received more than restoration.
She received a TESTIMONY.

She was the only one in that region that could say, *"My house was the feeding house while every other house was the needing house."*

She was the only woman that could carry that testimony.

6

PRINCIPLE 6
Confrontation and Demonstration

And it came to pass after many days (of the child alive, the meals multiplying), that the word of the Lord came to Elijah in the third year saying, "Go shew thyself unto Ahab; and I will send rain upon the earth."

1 Kings 18:1

Elijah was a man subject to like passions as we are, and he prayed earnestly that it might not rain; and it rained not on the earth by the space of three years and six months. And he prayed again, and the heaven gave rain, and the earth brought forth her fruit.

James 5:17

When Elijah prayed, the Word of the Lord came to him. When the Word comes, *it informs you of what is already a done deal.*

Out of the millions of people in the nation, only seven thousand did not bow the knee to idolatry. These are feeble statistics when you consider the sheer magnitude of their numbers. So it is fair to say, that by in large, most of the land had backslidden and was worshipping idols.

According to the word of the prophet, it hadn't rained in three years and six months. Things were looking very desperate.

And Ahab said unto Obadiah, "Go into the land, unto

all fountains of water, and unto all brooks, peradventure we may find grass to save the horses and mules alive, that we lose not all the beasts."

1 Kings 18:5

Ahab sent Obadiah to search for water. While Obadiah was on his way, Elijah met up with him. Upon seeing the prophet, Obadiah fell on his face in reverence. Elijah instructed him to go and to tell Ahab, *"Behold Elijah is here"* (1 Kings 18:8b).

And he (Obadiah) said, "What have I sinned, that thou wouldest deliver thy servant into the hand of Ahab, to slay me?"

1 Kings 18:9

Ahab had launched a national campaign to find Elijah, yet Elijah could not be found. During the famine, the king had unsuccessfully searched every nation and every kingdom for the prophet. He was always hidden from their sight. Consequently, Obadiah was afraid that the Spirit of the Lord would carry Elijah away as soon as he departed to find Ahab. He knew that if he returned with Ahab, and Elijah was gone, that it would cost him his life.

Elijah assured Obadiah that he would show himself to Ahab. It was the appointed time of confrontation and demonstration.

And it came to pass when Ahab saw Elijah, that Ahab said unto him, "Art thou he that troubleth Israel?" And he answered, "I have not troubled Israel; but thou, and thy father's house, in that ye have forsaken the commandments of the Lord, and thou hast followed Baalim. Now therefore send, and gather to me all Israel unto mount Carmel, and the prophets of Baal four hundred and fifty, and the prophets of the groves four

hundred, which eat at Jezebel's table."

1 Kings 18:17-19

Confrontation and Demonstration.

Elijah is a type of a generation...

...**that knows God.**
...**that will not be buried.**
...**that will be caught up.**
...**that will do signs and wonders.**
...**that will bring nations to their knees.**

Elijah is a type of **somebody that speaks a word that never fails.** He is a type and a shadow of a people that will rise up. He is a type of a prophetic generation that will go from one level of promotion, to another level of promotion, and then to a level of *confrontation.*

"Behold my God is Jehovah! Go bring your gods! Go bring your prophets! Go bring your idols and let us meet. It is time for us to have a supernatural confrontation! It is showdown time! It is time to see God's name exalted above every other name. It is revival time." How do you know Elijah? *"It is dry. The cattle and livestock are in peril. The nation is in famine."*

"Go tell him that 'My God is Jehovah' is here!"
"Go tell him, that I am present!"
"Go tell him, the Living God has spoken!"

When God speaks, IT IS A DONE DEAL.

"Go tell him that I want to meet him."
"Go tell him that there is rain coming!"
"Go tell him it is revival time."
"Although it is dry..."
"Although it is not flowing..."

"Although there are not many believing..."
"Although there are not many experiencing..."
*"**...the Word of God came to me.**"*

"Go tell him! I am about to inform him of that which has already taken place in the realm of the Spirit."

You are living in revival and restoration. There is an abundance of rain coming to the Earth. It is coming upon your life. It will revive and refresh, for its substance is all-inclusive. It carries supernatural supply for your life, your call and your destiny. The sound of abundance is very near. In fact, it is just overhead. Allow the sound to fill your heart with the expectation of Heaven for your life.

7

PRINCIPLE 7
Divine Help

And it shall come to pass, as soon as I am gone from thee, that *the Spirit of the Lord shall carry* **thee whither I know not; and so when I come and tell Ahab, and he cannot find thee, he shall slay me but I thy servant fear the Lord from my youth.**

1 Kings 18:12

The Spirit of the Lord shall carry thee. God is your source of DIVINE HELP. His presence and power will pick you up and take you to another place, *to another level.* You do not serve the God that you carry. You serve the God that carries you. His divine power provides upward mobility!

The wind of God has carried you. You did not get to this place in the Kingdom of God through the intelligence of man or through natural means. There was a wind - *a breath from Heaven that carried you.*

God not only carried you in the past, but He will carry you in the present. Where God is taking you, your intellect does not know. It is a place you have never been.

The one that is born of the Spirit is like the wind! You hear the sound of it, but you do not know where it is coming from or where it is going. It is the same with the person that is born of the Spirit. They blow with the winds of God.

The Spirit of the Lord shall carry you.

Revival time!

You are going to get carried away!
YOU ARE GOING TO GET CARRIED UP!
You are going to be elevated to another level!
You will see things from a divine perspective!

God is going to *raise you up*, *lift you up*, and *carry you*!

We do not serve the God that we carry.
We serve the God that CARRIES US.

We do not serve the God that we support.
We serve the God that SUPPORTS US.

We do not serve the God that we help.
We serve the God that HELPS US.

We do not serve the God that we build.
We serve the God that BUILDS US.

We do not serve the God that we shape or mold. He is not an idol that we have made! We serve a God that shapes us and molds us. He breathes on us by His Spirit and carries us.

Elijah had already experienced being carried by the Spirit. Wherever Ahab sent to find him, the Spirit of the Lord carried him away! The Spirit would lead him. The Spirit would reveal information ahead of time and the Spirit would carry him. He was supernaturally elusive!

You could not get a hold of him;
for he was supernaturally sustained.

You could not deprive him of the provision of God;
for he was supernaturally protected.

You could not destroy him or shut the words of his mouth;

for the Spirit was carrying him.

Elijah is a type of THIS GENERATION.

You do not get direction by bumping into things like a remote control car. It's not hit and miss! You are filled with the winds of God! **When the breath of the Spirit blows through you, He leads you with specific direction and carries you.**

Even the youths shall faint and be weary, and the young men shall utterly fall; But they that wait upon the Lord shall renew their strength; they shall mount up with wings as eagles; they shall run, and not be weary; and they shall walk, and not faint.

Isaiah 40:30-31

The Spirit is going to carry you.
SUPERNATURAL HELP!

Obadiah said, *"If I go now and tell Ahab, the Spirit will carry you."* The Spirit is not carrying you *away* from the confrontation. **The Spirit is carrying you to the confrontation!**

It is a different day. It is a day when **you will demonstrate the power of the God that carries you.** Everybody else serves the god that *they carry*. They serve the god that they shape. They worship the gods that they tote around. They bow down to the very things that they have created.

The One that is there to make His Word a done deal in your life, has sent you to **CONFRONT YOUR ADVERSARY** and to **DEMONSTRATE HIS POWER.**

The Spirit of the Lord is carrying YOU in this time of revival.
It's rain time!
It's ABUNDANCE time!

8

PRINCIPLE 8
The Day of Showing

And Elijah *(My God is Jehovah)* said, "As the Lord of hosts *(or the Captain of the Armies)* liveth before whom I stand, I will surely shew myself unto him today."

1 Kings 18:15

There is a day of showing.
It is called today.
It is a **demonstration** and **manifestation** day.

Thus saith the Lord:

TODAY IS A DAY of showing.
TODAY IS A DAY of demonstration.
TODAY IS A DAY of performance.
TODAY IS A DAY of the greater anointing.
TODAY IS A DAY of rain showers.
TODAY IS A DAY of…
…Visitation.
…Restoration.
…Abundance.
…Judgment to idols.
…Challenge to decision.

TODAY IS A DAY of change in the Earth.
TODAY IS A DAY of visitation for the planet.

TODAY IS A DAY
where *"My God who is Jehovah, liveth"*

will reveal Himself in the Name of Jesus
through the Body of Christ
with **SIGNS AND WONDERS**
like we have **NEVER SEEN** before.

TODAY IS THE DAY
that God will do in your life
what you are not prepared for!

He has been preparing you...
and He will continue to prepare you
to see what you are not prepared for.

Get your spirit ready for the superabundance
and THE MORE THAN ENOUGH because
it is on YOU right now!

In the previous chapters, God delivered you and set you free.

NOW God will *impact* you and *impart* to you.

9

PRINCIPLE 9
Revival Fire

In the life of Elijah, a day of spiritual confrontation came. It was a day of showing when Elijah confronted Ahab, the false prophets and all those that were unbelieving.

And it came to pass when Ahab saw Elijah, that Ahab said unto him, "Art thou he that troubleth Israel?" And he answered, "I have not troubled Israel; but thou, and thy father's house, in that ye have forsaken the commandments of the Lord, and thou hast followed Baalim. Now therefore send, and gather to me all Israel unto mount Carmel, and the prophets of Baal four hundred and fifty, and the prophets of the groves four hundred, which eat at Jezebel's table."

1 Kings 18:17-19

The life of Elijah is a type and a shadow of what God has reserved for this generation in this end-time. God will exhibit the power of His Word in your life. There will be a distinction in your life through the results experienced in the areas of faith and prayer.

There is a vast difference between those who *know God* and those who *know about God*. In these last days, God will make a distinction between those two groups.

**When THE WORD is a
<u>DONE DEAL</u> in
YOUR LIFE,**

You will **Confront Your Adversary.**
You will **Demonstrate God's Power.**

The Spirit will carry you.
Divine Help will be abundantly supplied.

It is a **Day of Showing.**
It is a **Day of Demonstration and Manifestation.**
It is a **Day of Revival.**
It is a **Day of God's Fire…**
…and you will *run* like never before.

When all of Israel and the prophets of Baal were gathered unto Mount Carmel, Elijah told those that did not serve Jehovah to build an altar and to make an offering to their god on it. Elijah, however, would build an altar to the Lord and make an offering to the one, true and Living God.

Confronting the multitude, he offered this ultimatum:

And call ye on the name of your gods, and I will call on the name of the Lord: and the God that answereth by fire, let him be God.

1 Kings 18: 24a

The prophets of Baal feverishly built their altar and prepared their offering. They called on Baal from morning until noon, beseeching him to answer. They jumped, danced, cut themselves and cried aloud, but the Bible records, *"But there was no voice, nor any that answered"* (1 Kings 18: 26b).

And Elijah said unto all the people, "Come near unto me." And all the people came near unto him. And he repaired the altar of the Lord that was broken down.

1 Kings 18: 30

Revival Fire

After Elijah rebuilt the altar of the Lord, he laid the offering upon the altar and had it doused with water three separate times. At the appointed hour, he approached the altar and prayed out loud before the multitudes, *"...let it be known this day that Thou art God in Israel and that I am Thy servant, and that I have done all these things at thy Word..."* (1 Kings 18:36b).

Then the fire of the Lord fell.

1 Kings 18:38a

Revival and Restoration

There is not a great mystery when there is a great revelation! God did not arbitrarily cause His fire to fall on Mount Carmel that day. He released that information *with* previous revelation. He gave a Word to His prophet.

God gives His Word to His remnant and to His people. He prepares us for what we have never seen. He prepares us so that what our eyes have never seen will not serve as the basis to disregard the impossible.

This is an hour where...
YOU will love God like never before!

It is a time where ...
YOU will experience victory that exceeds your expectations!

It is a time where...
YOU will do things that nobody thought you could do!

It is a time where...
YOU will rise up to levels that nobody dreamed possible!

You are not going to decline!
You are on the INCLINE!

Now unto Him that is able to do exceeding abundantly above all that we ask or think, according to the power that worketh in us.

Ephesians 3:20

It is the time when…
God will *restore* to you what the cankerworm has eaten.

It is the time when…
God will *erase* the memories of disappointments in the past.

It is the time when…
God will *increase* the treasure of your revelation.

It is YOUR time!

Nothing happened to the false prophets' offering. Their investment was on the wrong altar! Their confidence was in the wrong god! Elijah, *who had a done deal Word*, already knew that the false prophets were not going to be answered.

God is the FUEL of your life.

He is the God that is the **inspiration of your ministry.**
He is the God that is the **continuation of your call.**
He is the God that is the **preserver of your existence.**

He is your *Healer.*
He is your *Provider.*
He is your *Right Now*, your *Strength*, and your *Provision*.

This is your time of REVIVAL and RESTORATION!

Elijah repaired the altar of the Lord. Today, in many lives and in many churches, the altar of the Lord is broken up. It has been broken down by the double-minded and the unbelieving forces in the world. God, however, has sent me to repair the altar.

Elijah prepared an offering to the Lord. Then the fire of the Lord fell. Elijah said, *"Let the god that answers by fire, let Him be God."*

Elijah had never seen fire come down from Heaven! He had never witnessed such a thing with his eyes, but he had a Word from God! He knew that his God would perform. Elijah *repaired* and *prepared*. When the time came and he called on the name of the Lord, *the fire fell.*

From that day on, it was normal for Elijah to call down fire from Heaven! Second Kings describes another such incident. Elijah went to another level! A supernatural precedent was established in his life that set the stage for daily breakthrough and performance.

> WHAT YOU HAVE NEVER SEEN *WILL NOT ONLY HAPPEN,*
> BUT IT WILL BECOME YOUR EVERYDAY EXPERIENCE.
> IT WILL BECOME YOUR NORM.
> IT WILL BECOME YOUR REGULAR.

This is an appointed time for you!

You are in the middle of revival and restoration and the fire of God will burn bright in your life!

Listen to the Sound

And Elijah said unto Ahab, "Get thee up. Eat and drink, for there is a sound of abundance of rain."

1 Kings 18:41

Elijah...prayed earnestly that it might not rain; and it rained not on the earth by the space of three years and six months. And he prayed again, and the heaven gave rain, and the earth brought forth her fruit.

James 5:17b

You cannot separate rain from abundance. Rain brings abundance.

God is raising up an altar and preparing for Himself a generation that *hears* the sound of abundance.

THERE WILL BE ABUNDANCE
of love in your marriage.

THERE WILL BE ABUNDANCE
of love in your life.

THERE WILL BE ABUNDANCE
of blessing in your home.

THERE WILL BE ABUNDANCE
of finances in your life.

THERE WILL BE ABUNDANCE
of performance in your business.

THERE WILL BE ABUNDANCE
of direction in your steps.

THERE WILL BE ABUNDANCE
of fruit in your life.

THERE WILL BE ABUNDANCE!

You are **God's husbandry.** You are **God's field.** You are **God's earth.** You are **God's ground.** When God's rain comes down on you, there is **ABUNDANCE** in your life. It causes increase and overflow. It yields a never exhaustible supply of divine fruit. It is all-inclusive. It is comprehensive. You cannot contain its fullness for the overflow will overtake you.

What is the definition of abundance? It's A LOT!

Today, I hear the sound of <u>A LOT</u> in YOUR LIFE!

It is the *sound of abundance* in your life!
I hear the sound of what will not run out!

You are not reading this book by mere coincidence. You have been set up by Heaven; for today is a day of appointment and mobilization. You have been targeted by God for God's best!

LISTEN TO THE SOUND.

And Elijah went up to the top of Carmel and he cast himself down upon the earth, and put his face between his knees. And said to his servant, "Go up now, look toward the sea." And he went up, and looked, and said,

"There is nothing." And he said, "Go Again" seven times.

1 Kings 18:42b-43

There is not a cloud in the sky! There is no thunder, or even so much as a hint of lightning! The ground is dry from three years and six months of drought. There is no natural reason to expect rain in the forecast. All natural evidence points to dryness and decrease. Elijah, however, *hears the sound of abundance.*

What God is pouring out is GREATER than anything you have seen. The sound I hear is the sound of abundance. **I hear the sound of abundance in your life!**

When the fire of God falls, you can be sure that it will be accompanied by an outpouring of abundance. When God demonstrates that He is God in your life, you can be sure that there will be a sound of abundance. *You will hear the inaudible.* You will be convinced of the impossible because your information comes from a higher realm.

In the world today, there are many that are *talking about God.* They debate His nature. They debate His doings, but they do not know the one and only true God. Some of these are waiting for rain. There are others, however, *who hear it.* You cannot hear the inaudible if you have other voices in your ear.

I hear the sound of...
abundance!
I hear the sound of...
power that has been prepared for this hour.
I hear the sound of...
more than what you can use being poured on you.
I hear the sound of...
superabundance.
I hear the sound of...
what is not yet manifested.

I HEAR THE SOUND!

I hear **a sound that is so certain** that there is no time to tarry. Run *now* because it is going to *overtake* you!

It is a NOW sound.
It is raining now!

Before there are visible clouds, there are invisible clouds.
Before there is visible lightning, there is invisible lightning.
Before there is audible thunder, there is inaudible thunder.
Before you get wet physically, you get wet spiritually.

It is raining and you are in the middle of revival and restoration. God is pouring out His Spirit in order that the Earth would yield its fruit. Multitudes are being taken out of the world and into the Kingdom of Almighty God. *It is harvest time!*

I hear the sound of
Abundance!

10

PRINCIPLE 10
Run Like Never Before!

You are going to *hear* like you have never heard before!

You know what people are *hearing* by what people are *talking*. Listen to yourself. *How do you know what you are hearing?* It is what you are expecting. You will talk your convictions. You will speak what you hear. You will give sound to the voice that you are listening to.

I cannot make you expect what I am expecting. I can only give you the Word of the Lord for your life. In the end, YOU WILL DECIDE *what you hear*. You will decide what you expect and what you expect is what you are listening to. What you are listening to *is what you will hear*.

LISTEN!

Do you HEAR the sound?

It is the sound of
ABUNDANCE!

I hear the voice of the Spirit of God saying:

It is not devil time.
It is not anti-Christ time.
It is not poverty time.

It is not sickness time.
It is not defeat time.
It is not strife time.
It is not time for complacency.
It is not time for sorrow.
It is not time for failure.
It is not time for pain.
It is not time for double-mindedness.
It is not time for doubt fear and unbelief.
It is not time for mediocrity and inactivity.

It is MY TIME...
  to show Myself mighty
  in the lives of My people.

It is **abundance time.**
It is **action time.**
It is **time to act in God.**
It is **time to expect what is being poured out from above.**

YOU WILL BEAR MORE FRUIT at this hour than you have ever bore in your life. Your earth shall bring forth her fruit. The earth of your spirit shall bring forth abundance. **The good soil of your heart, where you have hid God's Word, will yield her increase.**

MY CHURCH IS GETTING OVER THE ASHES OF REPENTANCE. It will walk through the ashes of being sorry. It will get through the process of a final repentance. It will not halt and wobble between whom it will serve.

MY CHURCH WILL BE WEARING BEAUTY...
  ...*instead of ashes.*
    ...JOY *instead of mourning.*

MY CHURCH WILL BE WEARING...
  ...the *garments of praise.*
    ...instead of the spirit of heaviness.

**MY CHURCH WILL BE
A TREE OF RIGHTEOUSNESS...**
>...a tree of righteousness that *cannot be uprooted.*
>>...whose branches *cannot be fruitless.*

MY CHURCH WILL BE AS A CITY
>...BUILT ON A HILL.
>>**...Beautifully situated.**
>>>**...The joy of the whole Earth.**
>>>>...Mount Zion.

It will not be a Church that is
>...*raggedy* or *sick.*
>...*broke* or *defeated.*
>...*over-ridden* or *intimidated.*

My fire is going to burn out everything
THAT IS A HINDRANCE TO MY REALITY
in being an ever-present God.

SHOWERS *upon* SHOWERS *upon* SHOWERS
of visitation and restoration
>to take what used to be drought,
>and what used to be lack,
>and what used to be less than enough,
>AND OVERCOME IT
>**with the SUPERABUNDANCE
>of Almighty God.**

At this hour, YOUR LIFE WILL YIELD more fruit
than you have ever seen in your life!

THIS IS YOUR HOUR!

*The husband waits patiently
for the precious fruit of the earth.*

Predestined Glory

I HEAR THE SOUND of abundance!
The earth will bring forth her fruit.
The husbandman waits!
When it rains, IT POURS.

What is the husbandman waiting for?
He waits for the fruit of the earth.

What does the earth need?
The abundant rain that will produce the harvest

Every revival that we have seen, mankind has somehow managed to short-circuit. Instead of a down pouring, there have been showers. There is, however, the sound of abundance!

This one will not wane. This one will not stop.

This one **YOU will hear.** This one **YOU will see.**
and YOU will run like you have never run before!

This is not just to revive. *This is to restore.*

It will not restore to a former glory,
but to a **PREDESTINED GLORY.**

This is not just revival, but restoration. It's not a restoration into how good it used to be, but it's restoration into the image of Christ.

This is not about building the Church after the pattern of some great man of God in times past. This is about building the Church according to how Jesus builds it.

Upon this rock I will build My church and the gates of hell will not prevail against it.

Matthew 16:18

I HEAR THE SOUND OF ABUNDANCE!

We are not swimming in a puddle.
We are called to the depths of God's ocean.

God has only begun!

The Sound that Moves You

> Ask ye of the Lord rain in the time of the later rain.
>
> **Zechariah 10:1a**
>
> Elijah was a man subject to like passions as we are, and he prayed earnestly that it might not rain; and it rained not on the earth by the space of three years and six months.
>
> **James 5:17**

A man's prayer impacted the planet and changed a nation.

God wants you to understand that the times and the season that you live in, are the times and seasons that will bring GOD'S BEST to those who are tenacious. Prayer, therefore, is not a subject. It is an act. It requires a spiritual tenacity in the realm of the Spirit.

Are you a complainer or are you a transformer?
Are you called to complain about the drought...
...or are you called to call down the flood?

Elijah said, *"It is not only coming. It is coming so quickly that you better get in your chariot and GO NOW because I hear the sound of abundance of rain."*

GOD IS CALLING YOU TO HEAR
like you have never heard before.

My ear is not to the natural telephone. It is not to the horse's mouth. It is not to the grapevine or even to the ground. My ear is to *hear* what the Spirit is saying to the Church. I am not moved by newspaper headlines, but I am moved by a God who said, *"It is the hour of supernatural abundance."*

I hear the sound of abundance!

It is not *coming*.
IT IS HERE.

You are called by God to *hear* like I hear. You are called to hear like Elijah heard. You are called to hear what the Spirit is saying.

I hear *abundance* in the Church.
I hear *revival* across the Earth.
I hear *change* for the nations of the Lord.
I hear *resurrection* for the dead.
I hear *power* in the Church.
I hear *health* in your life.
I hear *wealth* in your business.
I hear *abundance of answers* to your prayers.

Remember, what you hear is determined by *who* you listen to. Where you look determines where you go. The sound will move you. *Listen and hear!*

So Ahab went up to eat and drink. And Elijah went up to the top of Carmel; and he cast himself down upon the earth, and put his face between his knees.

1 Kings 18:42

"I hear the sound of abundance!"
What are you going to do about it?

"I got a prophetic word from a prophet!"
What are you going to do about it?

"The Lord spoke to me in a dream about my call and destiny."
What are you going to do about it?

Are you going to sit there and wait for some season in the future? No, take hold of that thing and pray! That thing is not coming *some day*, but it is for the *right now*. Pray it into *fulfillment now*! Before you get out of your prayer chamber, it will be a done deal! Remember, those who believe the Word, will act on the Word.

And said to his servant, "Go up now, look toward the sea." And he went up, and looked, and said, "There is nothing." And he said, "Go again seven times."

1 Kings 18:43

Elijah did not need to go and look at the horizon because he had already heard the inaudible. He had already seen the invisible. He knew the cloud was coming. He heard the sound of abundance.

You are called to see what is coming.

Manifest Power

Before *devil-time,* there is *Church-time.* Before any anti-Christ has the right to show up, Christ in you the hope of glory will rise up. Your city will be shaken like it has never been shaken before.

A miraculous supernatural invasion of Almighty God is upon us! It is a revival that will take people who are going in one direction and turn them 360° in another direction. It is a yoke-breaking, burden-removing, addiction-eliminating, debt-canceling, finance-supplying, wealth-bringing, fire-igniting, revelation-imparting, gift-equipping revival of the Holy Ghost!

Men and women will rise up and break the powers of racism, dead denominationalism, and selfishness. They will rise up and manifest the power of the living Christ.

> GOD IS PREPARING YOU.
> GOD HAS BEEN PREPARING YOU
> AND GOD WILL CONTINUE PREPARING YOU
> TO SEE WHAT YOU HAVE NEVER EXPECTED.

The criminal is about to become the Christ-praiser.
The dealer is about to become the devil-exerciser.

The world has not yet known the power, the significance and the reputation of the living Christ. We are at the threshold of running into the wall of glory! Jesus Christ is about to stretch his hand of supernatural power over this world. His power will touch men, women and children. It will yank them out of the shackles of bondage and bring them into the House of God.

He is raising up an army. He is raising up a people.
HE IS BUILDING HIS CHURCH!

His name and His reputation will spread. No one will be able to put Him on the same pedestal with other dead gods. No one will put Him on *science's shelf*. No one will put him on the *educational* level. No one will put Him on the *emotional* level. No one will put Him on the *religious* level. Christ is going to show out! It is His time!

You are going to be strengthened to hear the sound of abundance of rain. He is going to give you acute hearing and accurate spiritual vision through the Word of God.

You were not born with wishes and desires that you dreamed up for yourself. He put those desires in you. **He gave you the dream!**

You are the head, not the tail.
You are going over, not under.
You are the lender, not the borrower.
You are the healer, not the sick.

Elijah heard the sound.
What do you do when you hear THE SOUND?

You are not under the circumstance. You are not a prisoner. Your hands are not tied. God has given YOU the keys of the Kingdom of Heaven and YOU have the authority to bind and loose. You can run the race without having to quit, waiver or stop. The greatest power in the universe is available to you through the power of the indwelling of Christ.

Work What You Hear

And Elijah said unto Ahab, "Get thee up, eat and drink, for there is a sound of abundance of rain."

1 Kings 18:41

And it came to pass in the mean while, that the heaven was black with clouds and wind, and there was a great rain...And the hand of the Lord was on Elijah and he girded up his loins, and ran...

1 Kings 18:45a-46a

This abundance of rain was the fulfillment of a prophetic word that was birthed through prayer.

WORK what you hear in the Spirit. WORK the promises.

When you do not see the cloud, it is still there.

Do you hear the cancellation of debt? **Start thanking God.**

Do not sit and wear a sorrowful face when you have heard the sound of abundance in your life. *Work it!* It is not for another season. This is the season! It is for this time in your life.

The little cloud might not look impressive at first, but don't let that stop you! If you hesitate, you will fall behind. Therefore, RUN FAST because what you see is not *a little*. It is about to fill the sky. What fills the sky will pour out in abundance.

You are going to hear like you have never heard.
You are going to see like you have never seen.

One moment it was just a benign little cloud in the horizon. All of a sudden, the sky was black with clouds and the heavens opened. God's supernatural will not take a decade or a century to happen in your life. God did not bring you this far to leave you!

God is *not* powerless.
God is *not* absent or mysterious.

God is not the God that you help.
He is the God that helps you!

God is not the God that you support.
He is the God that supports you!

God is not the God that you carry.
He is the God that carries you!

The HAND OF THE LORD came on Elijah and he *RAN!*

God has prepared you to **SEE** like you have never seen.
God has prepared you to **HEAR** like you have never heard.
God has prepared you to **RUN** like you have never run.

GET READY TO RUN!
This revival is not coming, *it is here!*

Look and see! Hear the Sound!
It's the size of a man's hand.
ABUNDANCE is on the horizon!
It is upon us **NOW!**

And the skies are filling with the cloud of God's glory.

CHAPTER 11
I Hear the Sound of Abundance!

You are living in the time of revival and restoration. God will refresh, renew, revive, resurrect, and strengthen you. He will RISE UP IN YOU and RAISE YOU UP. He will take you higher! Revival will cause the Body of Christ to stand. Revival will cause the Body of Christ to awaken. It will awaken unto righteousness and unto the works of Christ.

Revival will awaken you to God's purpose and priority. Revival will refresh. It will bring times of refreshing and strengthen the *spirit, soul and body*. Revival will resurrect purpose and priority in your life. It will cause you to understand that in prioritizing God, *you are not excluded*. When you put the Kingdom of God first, all things will be added unto you.

Revival can touch a people and then after awhile, as they disperse in thought and they contradict in confession, they will disunite in direction. Revival can wane, but restoration is reserved for a corporate generation.

Jesus does not have good days *and* bad day. He does not have great days *and* sad days. His days are packed with the faithfulness of His nature! Jesus only has great days! As a child of God, you have His nature and you are living in the fullness of *His day*. You are living in revival and restoration.

Martin Luther had a revelation and he nailed it to the church door. *"The just shall live by faith."* How is it possible that the Church waited so long for a revelation that was so elementary? Why did it then take until the early 1900's for the Body of Christ to embrace the Baptism of the Holy Ghost? In the 1950's, we had eleven years of the great healing revival. There were eleven years of the greatest demonstrations of miracles we had ever seen! There were eleven years where blind eyes were opened to the tune of five and six a night, and then suddenly, the momentum dropped off. Just like in times past, *the revival waned.* Why is that? What happened to the momentum?

Man tampered with the move of God. Men and women got in the way and diluted it. They interfered with the move of God because they were not prepared to carry revival out into restoration. When that happens, revival will wane until another revival comes.

You are not called to mediocrity. God's priority is corporate. In the past, we thought it was the believer's voice or the individual's voice. **This, however, is a corporate call to a prophetic destiny.**

You are not the only one on the planet. You are not alone. Elijah thought that he was the only one, but God had reserved for him seven thousand prophets who had not kissed the image of Baal.

> **Yet I have left, Me seven thousand in Israel all the knees which have not bowed unto Baal, and every mouth which hath not kissed him.**
>
> **1 Kings 19:18**

"Seven" is the number of God. "Seven" is the number of completion. "Thousand" is the largest number in the Bible. The Bible never mentions millions. It mentions "thousands and thousands," which ends up being more than millions. "Thousands" is a biblical number. **It is a remnant.**

So, it is the same with today's generation. God has reserved you and millions of others like you around the Earth. He has chosen and specifically called a corporate body of people that will work in power. God will show you what you have never seen!

He will use you like you have never been used before. He will give you what you have never had. God has a plan for your life.

This is the day of the corporate body of people. No one will be able to stop this revival, for it is a revival of restoration. It will not wane. It will not fade and man will not be able to put a label on it.

God will not stop until you have more than enough. God will not stop until you are ready to run a little more. God is coming for a Church that is victorious. He is coming for a Church that is fighting the good fight. The good fight is the fight that you are winning! When you are winning, you are having too much fun!

The Hour of Outpouring

"...for there is a sound of abundance of rain."

1 Kings 18:41b

When rain falls abundantly, it makes a sound. All the prophet could hear was rain! It was the sound of abundance!

Everything that comes out of the Earth to bless man is impacted and nourished with an abundant rainfall. It brings every blessing that man needs.

And the hand of the Lord was on Elijah; and he girded up his loins, and ran...

1 Kings 18:46a

When rain came, God's hand was upon it.
The moment the outpouring falls, His hand is on you!

You are going to run like you have never run. You are going to run with supernatural ability. His hand will be on you and you will be a radical runner for the King of Kings and the Lord of Lords. You will be a trailblazer for the Kingdom of God!

The hand of the Lord will be on you! It is the anointing. It is the mantle. It is the touch of God. Elijah saw it, spoke it and walked into it. When he did, the hand of the Lord came upon him.

See it, speak it and walk into it. Remember, there is a *response* to outpouring. When you believe the Word, you will act on the Word. You will work the Word.

The Hour of Outpouring

ASK YE of the Lord rain in the time of the latter rain; so the Lord shall make bright clouds, and give them showers of rain, to every one grass in the field.

Zechariah 10:1

Bright clouds, showers of rain, grass in the field – this is the perfect portrait of abundance. It is a land that has been revived and restored. It is a land that has been richly supplied with the brightness of God's glory and the abundance of Heaven's rain.

There is no one overlooked under this message. This prophetic word does not need your name on it because *it has your name on it.* It is for you today.

I hear the sound of abundance. It is the time of the latter rain. There is a great outpouring and the hand of the Lord is on you. As a remnant, you are going to run like you have never run before.

You are going to run out of debt.
You are going to run into wealth.

You are going to run out of strife.
You are going to run into love.

You are going to run out of weakness.
You are going to run into strength.

You are going to run out of sickness.
You are going to run into health.

You are going to run out of confusion.
You are going to run into accuracy.

You are going to run out of memories of fear and doubt.
You are going to run into power.

You are going to run as an example to others. You are going

to run as you take somebody by the hand. God is going to give you the ability to respond to the outpouring of Heaven. Your life is going to resemble a runner with a testimony. You are going to run in the streets proclaiming, *"Christ is coming! Revival is here! Restoration is coming!"* **You will herald the message and run like never before.**

The latter rain never comes before the former. The latter rain comes in the latter. When it comes, the hand of the Lord comes on you and there is grass in the field.

Together on the Frontline

Supernatural divine recognition of the time will be given to God's people. **We must know what time it is!**

For a corporate result, we need to ask with *one voice*. We have to live in *one mind* and with *one confession*. How can we experience the corporate result if the Body of Christ is individually divided by confession, distrust, gossip, and division? It is important for us to care about the connection that we have with one another.

You belong to a Body made up of multiplied millions. You are one of the ones who have chosen to take God and His Word at face value. You serve the God who will do the impossible. You serve a God of creative power! He is the God of resurrection life and of *uncapped supernatural abundance*!

Your God will never fail to do what He has promised to do! You are part of a championship family made up of men and women of every walk of life who have been anointed by the power of the Holy Ghost. You are on the wining team and Jesus is your Captain. Rejoice in the experience of it!

**What is prophecy and promise
WILL BECOME PERFORMANCE
in this hour that we are living in!**

There is a move of God made up of people. If you want to be on the frontline, you have to know the time. Together with the remnant, you have to ask *corporately* – with one heart and one mind.

But now I will not be unto the residue of this people as in the former days, saith the Lord of hosts. For the seed shall be prosperous; the vine shall give her fruit,

> **and the ground shall give her increase, and the heavens shall give their dew; and I will cause the remnant of this people to possess all these things.**
>
> Zechariah 8:11

These remnant people, who have the knowledge of the truth, will have access to the God of increase. God is talking to the remnant. *What is the remnant?* The remnant is the "seven thousand." It's the number of *God's completeness*. It is *everyone* that God has called. *It is everyone that has CHOSEN TO BE CHOSEN.*

The day has come when a corporate people will know what time it is. The day has come when a corporate generation will know the hour of the latter rain. The day has come when the remnant will ask of God corporately. There will be bright clouds, showers of rain and grass in *every* field.

I hear the Spirit of the Lord saying to you:

YOU ARE AT THE PLACE in time…
when I have released My revelation knowledge
to you in **GREAT ABUNDANCE.**

You are willing to receive it.
Now, **I WILL PERFORM** it in your life.

YOU ARE PART OF A GENERATION *like no other.*

YOU WILL HAVE
Earth's supply and **Heaven's dew.**

YOU WILL HAVE
Earth's fruit and **Heaven's rain.**

YOU WILL HAVE
Earth's favor and **Heaven's blessings.**

YOU WILL HAVE
it all and you will possess it all...
because **YOU** are living in this time!

Laugh in the Rain

> Be glad then, ye children of Zion, and rejoice in the Lord your God; for he hath given you the former rain moderately, and he will cause to come down for you the rain, the former rain, and the latter rain in the first month.
>
> Joel 2:23

The Lord is your Pavilion, your Tower, your Protection and your Shield.

Rejoice in the fact that your shield cannot be penetrated.
Rejoice in the fact that your supply will never run out.
Rejoice in the fact that you have the victory.
Rejoice in the fact that you live in corporate supply.
Rejoice IN THE SOUND OF ABUNDANCE!

When you are fortified in this, you will laugh at the threats. Every lie from the devil is powerless against the truth in God. It cannot penetrate your shield! Your power is greater. Your supply is all-inclusive. You are part of a chosen generation. You have been called by God to do exploits. This is the hour of your prophetic release. The atmosphere is filled with the sound of abundance. The rain is here. Therefore, be glad then! Laugh at every fiery dart, every negative thought and every doubt that is deflected off of your shield.

Do you HEAR it NOW?
The sound is very near.
It is the sound of
ABUNDANCE!

Laugh in the rain.
IT IS TIME.

**REVIVAL and RESTORATION
RUN** *like never before!*

And I will restore to you the years that the locust hath eaten, the cankerworm, and the caterpillar, and the palmerworm, my great army which I sent among you. And ye shall eat in plenty, and be satisfied, and praise the name of the Lord your God, that hath dealt wondrously with you; and my people shall never be ashamed.

Joel 2:25-25

YOUR PROPHETIC WORD
by Dr. Christian Harfouche

As you choose to accept My Abundance...
and to hear the sound of My prophetic
promise and to immerse yourself in
My will for you, I will bring to pass
in your life,
goodness and fulfillment never
seen before...
Blessings - spirit, soul and body...
and ABUNDANT RESOURCES
will overtake and overwhelm you
at this time...
your Day of vindication, transformation
and restoration is here...
My Hand is on you today for Daily
Performance. Your life as you
have known it, is now interrupted
by the life that you have never
known before...
Prepare your heart and say, "Yes!"
to what is greater and more rewarding.
For this is your time to see
My goodwill for you become
YOUR EXPERIENCE.
... Says the Spirit of the Lord
your time of the greater anointing
has come!

ABOUT THE AUTHOR

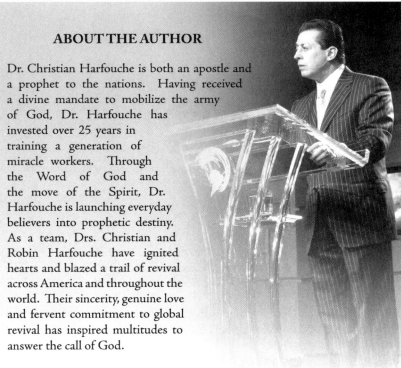

Dr. Christian Harfouche is both an apostle and a prophet to the nations. Having received a divine mandate to mobilize the army of God, Dr. Harfouche has invested over 25 years in training a generation of miracle workers. Through the Word of God and the move of the Spirit, Dr. Harfouche is launching everyday believers into prophetic destiny. As a team, Drs. Christian and Robin Harfouche have ignited hearts and blazed a trail of revival across America and throughout the world. Their sincerity, genuine love and fervent commitment to global revival has inspired multitudes to answer the call of God.

Drs. Christian and Robin Harfouche are committed to training New Testament disciples at The World Center in Pensacola, Florida. The World Center is home to both the International Miracle Institute Bible Training Center and a vibrant, multi-cultural, cross-denominational church. People from around the world move to Pensacola for training and impartation from a major miracle ministry. Drs. Christian and Robin Harfouche continue to travel worldwide, conducting Miracle Soul-Winning Crusades and imparting their lives to the Body of Christ. Their influence and the miracle testimonies of their disciples can be seen daily on the highly acclaimed television program, *Miracles Today*.

International Miracle Institute (IMI)
Equipping A Generation Of Miracle–Workers!

The Lord has given Drs. Christian and Robin Harfouche a mandate to train and equip over 400,000 miracle–workers for the great end–time harvest of souls.

Through the integrity of the Word of God and the move of the Spirit, IMI is empowering a generation to live in victory and to walk in power.

Invest yourself in a supernatural training program.

Allow revelation from the Word of God and impartation from a major miracle ministry to supernaturally equip you for your end–time purpose!

IMI offers two training options!

IMI In–Residence Training (Pensacola, Florida)
IMI Correspondence Program (home study program)

IMI Training At A Glance

- Receive training by Drs. Christian and Robin Harfouche.
- Grow in a practical revelatory understanding of the Word of God.
- Learn how to have continual supernatural results in God.
- Impact the world with signs, wonders and miracles following.
- Fully accredited to confer both undergraduate and graduate degrees.

For More Information:
Visit: www.globalrevival.com
Email: IMI@globalrevival.com
Phone: 850–439–6225

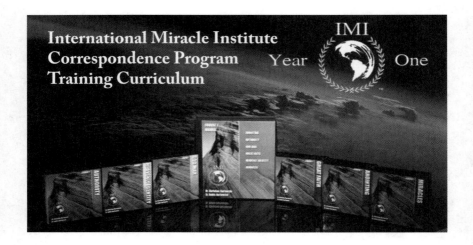

Year One of IMI powerfully equips those called to walk on the cutting edge in the Word of God. This foundation enables you as a believer to live and operate in the supernatural and fulfill the call of God on your life. **Year One is an accredited year of bible college, containing over 100 hours of teaching on 96 CD's.**

Your Authority:
Become all that you can be by knowing, understanding, and exercising your authority in Jesus Christ.

Heavenly Identity:
Understand your identity in Christ.

The God Man:
Learn all about the unlimited abilities invested in you.

Great Faith:
Find out how you can grow to be a wonder worker by building your faith in God.

The Anointing:
Find out about the Anointing in you and how you can cooperate with this unction.

Miracles:
Step into a place in the Lord where nothing is impossible.

Year Two of IMI continues where Year One left off, helping you unlock the deep truths and revelation in the Word of God. Building on the foundation of Year One, **Year Two further enables you as a believer to live and operate in the supernatural** and fulfill the call of God on your life. **Year Two is an accredited year of bible college, also containing over 100 hours of teaching on 96 CD's.**

Advanced Studies in Faith:
A study to build your faith from level to level.

Understanding the Supernatural:
Learn to operate in the highest dimension of life in the spirit.

Healing in the Atonement:
Understand your divine right to the provision and benefits of healing in the atonement.

Ministry Gifts:
"And God gave gifts unto men…" A study of the Call-The Office.

Prophets and Prophecy:
A study of Old and New Testament Prophets; recognize the spirit of error, develop the spirit of pioneer, study the predictive future Word, and learn to cooperate with the Anointing.

Demons & Demonology:
Understand the origin, operation, strategies, and the believers' dominion over the powers of darkness.

Remember, miracles don't just happen. By the Word of God and the power of the Spirit, the IMI Correspondence Program will train and equip you to be a miracle worker for this end-time harvest of souls.

"Study to show yourself approved unto God, a workman that needs not to be ashamed, rightly dividing the Word of Truth." 2 Timothy 2:15

For More Information:
Visit: www.globalrevival.com
Email: IMI@globalrevival.com
Phone: 850-439-6225

**For additional teaching resources
by Dr. Christian Harfouche
please visit us on the web at www.globalrevival.com**

or contact:

Global Revival Distribution
421 North Palafox St., Pensacola, Florida 32501
Email: info@globalrevival.com
Order Line: 850–439–9750

Real people living extraordinary lives – Miracle's Today celebrates the voice of the disciple. Televised daily around the world, Miracles Today captures the passion and purpose of a generation with a divine mandate. Embracing the promises of God and the triumphant walk of faith, Miracle's Today is the celebration of unscripted victories and real life miracle testimonies. Trained and mentored by Drs. Christian and Robin Harfouche, these disciples have answered a global call to broadcast the creative expression of God throughout the Earth. Miracle's Today is God's method of stirring a generation into destiny.

For broadcast times and stations, please visit:

www.globalrevival.com

For further information:
Christian Harfouche Ministries
421 N. Palafox St. • Pensacola, FL 32501

Office: 850–439–6225

Website: www.globalrevival.com
Email: info@globalrevival.com